ELECTROPLATER FIRST YEAR MCQ

OBJECTIVE QUESTION ANSWERS

MANOJ DOLE

Digitization is the need of the time. In the future, training in industrial training institutes will need to be conducted using online internet to make training more convenient and easy. E-books containing a set of MCQ questions will be made available to the trainees as they need to be more accustomed to the multiple choice questions MCQ to prepare for the online exams taking place in their industrial training institutes.

With all these factors in mind, Mr. Manoj Madhukar Dole Instructor, Industrial Training Institute, Satara, has written books according to the new annual system and NSQF-5 syllabus. And they've created theoretical mobile apps and blogs to make training easier, and made all these educational materials available for download on the world famous websites Google Play Store, Amazon and Apple Book Store.

The books were published by Hon'ble Joint Director Shri Rajendra Ghume Saheb Regional Office of Vocational Education and Training, Pune on 9/1/2019, at this time Shri Prakash Saigavkar Saheb Principal Government Industrial Training Institute Aundh Pune, Shri Tukaram Misal Saheb Principal Govt. Q. Sanstha Satara, Shri Sachin Dhumal Saheb District Vocational Education and Training Officer Satara, Shri Yatin Pargaonkar Saheb Principal Govt. Q. Sanstha Kolhapur, Shri Vikas Teke Saheb Inspector Vocational Education and Training Regional Office Pune, Palekar Foods Products Pvt. Ltd. Entrepreneurial Chairman of Satara Mr. Nilkanthrao Palekar Saheb, Chairman of Hira Foods Mr. Ibrahim Baba Tamboli Saheb, Mrs. Shalmali Pawar Headmaster Government Technical School Center Satara and other dignitaries were present on the occasion.

Contents

Prologue

Electroplater First Year MCQ is a simple Book for ITI & Engineering Course Electroplater First Year, Revised NSQF Syllabus, It contains objective questions with underlined & bold correct answers MCQ covering all topics including all about the latest & Important about safety and environment, use of fire extinguishers and various safety measures involved in the industry. He gets the idea of trade tools &machineries, practices on filing, hack sawing, planning, drilling, marking, cutting and chipping etc. Identifies different types of conductors, cables, prepare wire joints and learns crimping and soldering. Knowledge of basic electrical laws like Kirchhoff's law, ohm's law, laws of resistances and their applications. The trainee learns installation, testing and maintenance of batteries and wiring of panels. The trainee gets the idea of basic process of electroplating. The trainee learns to handle different solutions, treatment of hazardous chemicals, safety precautions in electroplating shop, first aid and antidotes for chemical poisoning. Preparation of articles before plating, different types of cleaning like polishing, buffing, blasting, electro-cleaning, ultrasonic cleaning and vapour degreasing etc. Skilling practice on Nickel and Bright & Hard Chromium plating by different methods, various defects generally encountered in plating, causes for these defects, their remedies and various methods to remove defective deposits. And lots more.

We add new question answers with each new version. Please email us in case of any errors/omissions. This is arguably the largest and best e-Book for All engineering multiple choice questions and answers.

As a student you can use it for your exam prep. This e-Book is also useful for professors to refresh material.

Foreword

Vocational education and training is imparted through the Department of Vocational Education and Training through the Department of Business Education and Business Practical to supply multi-skilled artisans in line with the rapidly growing demand in the industrial sector in the 21st century. All the occupations within the institutions are important, as the trainees from these occupations develop multi-skills as per the demands of the industry.

with the noble intention of making available MCQ e-books suitable for all businesses, considering that all the examinations in all the industries in the industrial sector are conducted online and include MCQ method questions. Mr. Manoj Madhukar Dole has written a very good e-book on MCQ method as per the new annual syllabus. This e-book will definitely be a guide for all the trainees, trainee candidates, training instructors and others concerned.

The author of the book is Mr. Manoj Madhukar Dole, Instructor Gov. ITI Satara has 17 years of training experience. Written as a new annual pattern, this e-book incorporates modern digital QR Code technology to understand the layout, simple language, and simple syntax, diagrams and videos for each subject. So I am sure that this e-book will definitely be useful for in-depth study and exam practice. The work they have done is certainly commendable.

Mr. Tukaram Misal
Principal Government Industrial Training Institute Satara.

Foreword

Vocational education and training is important [illegible] the Department of Vocational Education and Training [illegible] the Department of Business Education and Business Practice [illegible] supply qualified [illegible] in line with the rapidly growing demand in the industrial sector [illegible] important as the [illegible] development [illegible] of the industry.

[illegible]

Preface

DGET New Delhi and CSTARI Kolkata have been implementing an annual pattern for all businesses in ITI since the August 2018 session. The examination system will also be changed and it will be online from this year and since all the questions are of Objective Type (MCQ), the trainees are in dire need of in-depth study. It is with this in mind that we are delighted to present the books based on the old NIMI pattern and a complete overview of the new annual pattern, and we hope that these books will be a guide for all business directors and trainees. Is.

For writing these books, Johar Awate Saheb, Principal of ITI Akluj. Former Principal of ITI Satara Saigavkar Saheb, Assistant Director Shri Chandrakant Dhekne Saheb Regional Office of Vocational Education and Training, Pune, District Vocational Education and Training Officer Sachin Dhumal Saheb and Headmaster Government Technical School Kendra Shalmali Pawar Madam and son Adhiraj Dole, mother Kusum Dole, I am very grateful to my father Madhukar Dole and wife Ashwini Dole for their special guidance and cooperation from time to time.

Also, in a very short period of time, the book was reviewed by Shri Rajendra Ghume Saheb, Joint Director, Vocational Education and Training Regional Office, Pune, for his invaluable time in publishing the book. I am sincerely grateful for their feedback.

I am grateful to the Instructor of ITI Satara for there continuous support from the very beginning of writing the book.

From this book, I consider myself blessed to have shared my thoughts on e-learning with you. I will not claim that this book is perfect, because considering the perfection, this book is an attempt and is in its infancy. They will be valuable for improvement if they are tested and suggested.

Manoj Dole
Dated 9/1/2019

Acknowledgements

The industrial training and theoretical examination system of our industrial training institutes and these changes have been accepted by the craft instructors and the trainees. Theoretical examinations conducted in your industrial training institutes are also conducted online. Since these examinations are of multiple choice MCQ method, the trainees will need to get more practice of such questions.

With all these considerations in mind, Mr. Manoj Madhukar, Director, Dole Crafts, Katari Industrial Training Institute, Satara, has done a thorough study and with his diligent work and added his keen intellect, according to the new annual system and NSQF-5 syllabus, e-book of Katari and other machine trades. -Book) and they have created mobile apps and blogs on theoretical topics to make training easier and have made all these educational materials available for download on the world famous websites Google Play Store, Amazon and Apple Book Store. Training has been made easier by creating a print version and using advanced techniques like QR Code.

All these educational materials will definitely be a guide for all the trainees for in-depth study and for the craft instructors and other concerned who are imparting vocational training.

ACKNOWLEDGMENTS

CHAPTER ONE

Electroplater First Year QR Code Images

Download App
Online Test Exam
ITI Books
AutoCAD CAM
JOB & Apprentice
Online Theory
Computer Course
Trading Course
CNC Course
MSCIT Course
Shopping Business
Internet Business
Web Designing
Online Services
Top Sportsmans
Indian Army
Freedom Fighters
Top Scientists
Social Reformers
Motivational Speaker
Top Richest People
Join WhatsApp Group
Join Facebook Group
Like Facebook Page
PAN / Adhar / Licence Passport

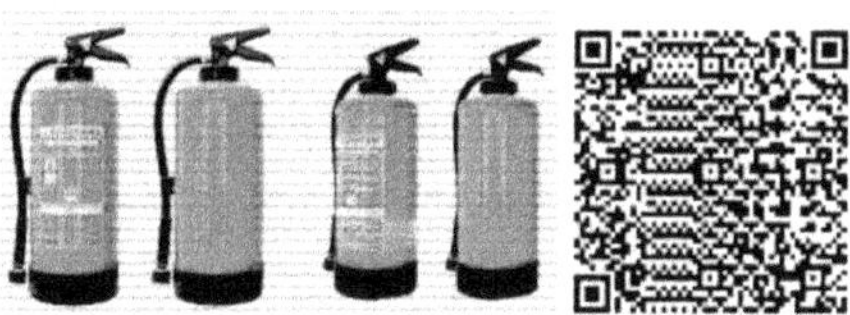

Fire extinguisher

Calliper

Hacksaw frame

Universal surface guage

Hammer

Centre punch

Bench vice

Files

Scraper

Surface Plate

Outside Micrometer

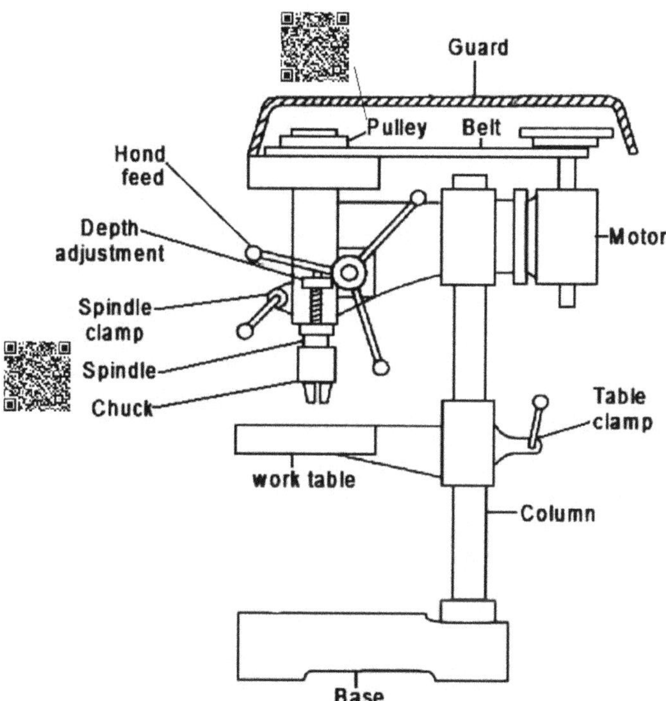

Piller Drilling Machine

Bench Grinding Machine

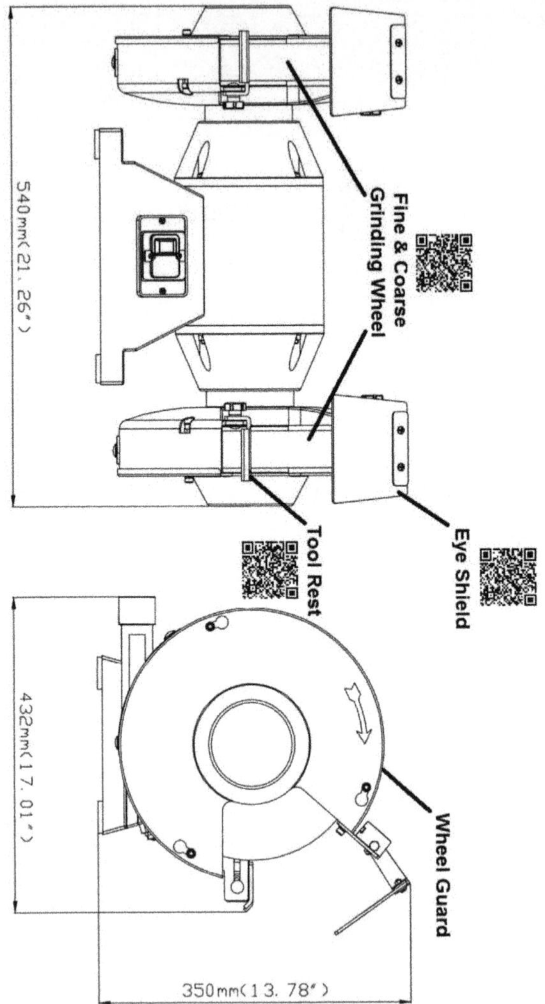

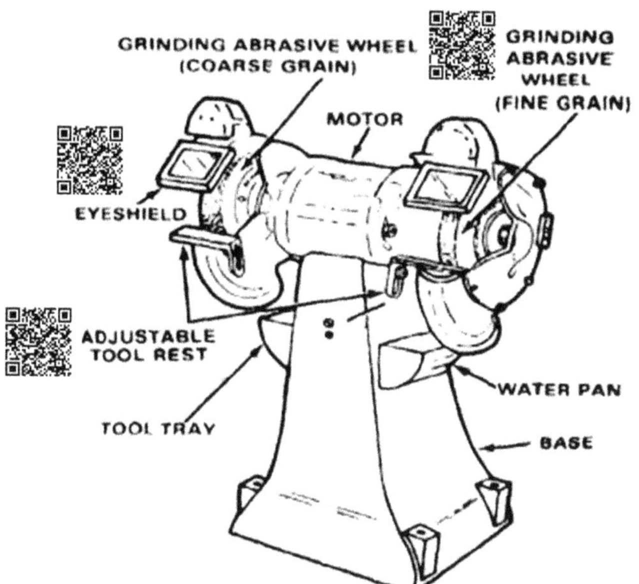

Pedastal Grinding Machine

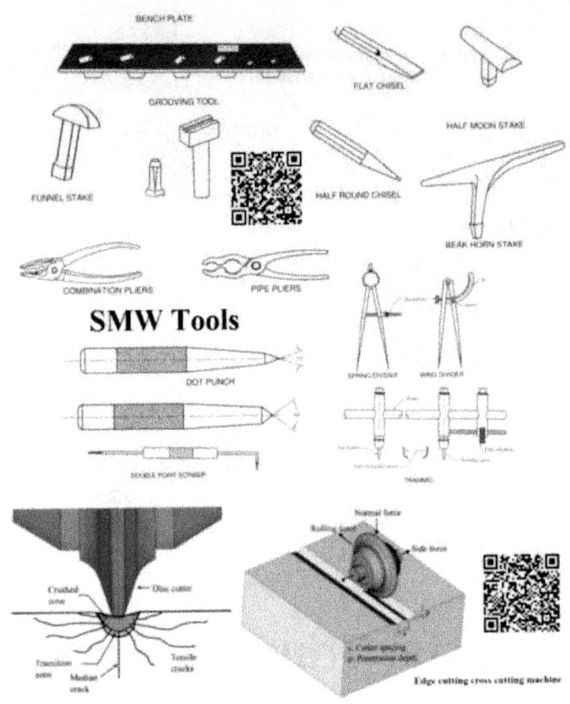
BENCH PLATE
FLAT CHISEL
GROOVING TOOL
HALF MOON STAKE
FUNNEL STAKE
HALF ROUND CHISEL
BEAK HORN STAKE
COMBINATION PLIERS
PIPE PLIERS
SMW Tools
DOT PUNCH
TRAMMEL
Normal force
Rolling force
Side force
Crushed zone
Disc cutter
Transition zone
Median crack
Tensile cracks
Edge cutting cross cutting machine

14 ITI Book MCQ - Manoj Dole
www.itibook.com
battery
capacitor
cell
dynamometer
electromagnet
heater
inductance
magnet
www.itigov.blogspot.com www.jobapprentices.blogspot.com www.ititests.blogspot.com
www.itibook.com

ITI Book MCQ - Manoj Dole
www.itibook.com
megger
motor
multimeter
ohmmeter
resistores
star connected alternator
voltmeter ammeter
wattmeter
www.itigov.blogspot.com
www.jobapprentices.blogspot.com
www.ititests.blogspot.com
www.itibook.com

CHAPTER TWO

Electroplater First Year MCQ

1] Which one is a workshop safety?

A] Keep shop floor clean and free from grease, oil or other slippery materials

B] Stop the machine before changing the speed

C] Don't use cracked or chipped tools

D] Don't try to stop a running machine with hand

2] In Personal Protect Equipment (PPE] HELMET is used to

A] protect head

B] Protect eyes

C] Protect hands

D] Protect ears

3] Which of the following belongs to general safety?

A Have a worker in good attitude

B] The work clean and clear

C] Concentrate on your work

D] Keep the floor and gangways clean and clear

4] While grinding, which is used to protect the eyes?

A] Dark green glass

B] Mask

C] Sun glasses

D] Safety goggles

5] Which of the following is done for machine safety?

A] Check the oil level before starting the machine

B] Do things in a methodical way

C] Keep the floor and gangways clean and clear

D] Don't use dies and scarves

6] ln Personal Protect Equipment (PPE], 'sleeves' is used to protect ----------

A] Face
B] Eyes
C] Ears
D] Hands
7] ABC stands for --------------
A] Automatic Breathing Control
B] Automatic Blood Control
C] Airway Breathing Circulation
D] Automatic Blood Circulation
8] Fire & FIRE EXTINGUISHERS

Fire extinguisher

9] To put off"Class B" fire, the types of fire extinguisher used is ....
A] dry power
B] Carbon dioxide
C] Jet of water
D] Foam type
10] Which type of fire extinguisher is used to put off general fire?
A] Water type Extinguisher
B] Foam type Extinguisher
C] Dry chemical powder Extinguisher
D] Carbon dioxide (C02] Extinguisher
11] In case of bleeding, take treatment Of
D] cold 3" and rest
A] spray cold water
B] Bandage immediately -----.
B] Enquire about the accident thought treatment

12] in case of an accident, the victim should im

A] Asked to take rest

C] Attended immediately

D] leave him

13] First aid is given to an injured or ill person primarily....

A] Save life

B] Prevent further deterioration of the muff's

C] Give best possible comfort

D] All of these

14] Colour code for Bins for waste paper segregation is -----

A] blue Colour

B] Yellow Colour

C] Red Colour

D] Green Colour

15] In Japanese Seiko stands for --------------

A] Shine

B] Sort

C] Standardize

D] Sustain

16] Benefit of SS system is ------

A] Increase in productivity

B] Increase in quality

C] Reduction in wastage of time

D] All of these

17] Safety is -----------

A] nobody's business

B] every bodise business

C] Some bodies business

D] The organization business

18] For basic categories of safety signs are available The meaning of"prohibition" sign ----

A] shows it must not be done
B] Shows what must be done
C] Warns the hazard or danger
D] Gives information of safety provision

18] One micrometer (U] is equal to...
A] 0.1mm
B] 0.01mm
C] 0.001mm
D] 0.0001mm

19] The caliper meant for measuring the width of a slot is...
A] Odd leg caliper
B] Outside caliper
C] Jenny caliper
D] Inside calliper

Calliper

20] The size of the dividers are specified by the -----------
A] Total length of legs
B] Distance between the points when fully opened
C] Length of legs without points
D] distance between the pivot and the point

21] The instrument used to mark parallel lines, parallel to the datum edge is -
A] jenny caliper
B] Divider
C] Outside calliper
D] Inside calliper

22] Which one of the following is an indirect measuring tool?
A] Outside caliper
B] Vernier calliper
C] Steel rule

D] Outside micrometer

23] For cutting thin tubing, the most suitable pitch of the hacksaw blade is...

A] 1.8mm

B] 1.4mm

C] 1mm

D] 0.8mm

24] For cutting solid brass, the most suitable pitch of the hacksaw blade is...

A] 1.8mm

B] 1.4mm

C] 1mm

D] 0.8mm

Hacksaw frame

25] A new hacksaw blade after a few strokes becomes loose because of the...

A] Stretching of the blade

B] Wing-nut threads being worn out

C] Wrong pitch of the blade

D] Improper selection of the set of saws.

26] While cutting small diameter pipes, it is advisable to watch regularly and ensure that...

A] The cut is along the curved line

B] More saw teeth are in contract

C] The work is not overheated

D] Proper balancing of hacksaw is maintained

27] The vice clamps are used to...

A] Protect hard jaws

B] Clamp the work pieces rigidly

C] Protect the finished surfaces

D] Prevent the movable jaw being filed

28] The reference surface during marking is provided by the...

A] Surface gauge

B] Workpiece

C] Drawing of the work

D] Marking table surface

29] The size of an engineer's vice is specified by the...

A] Length of the movable jaw

B] Width of the jaws

C] Height of the vice

D] Maximum opening of the jaws

30] The part of the universal surface gauge which helps to draw a parallel line along a datum edge is the..

A] Rocker arm

B] Snug

C] Fine adjustment screw

D] Guide pins

Universal surface guage

31] Scribers are made of...

A] Mild steel

B] High carbon steel

C] Brass

D] Cast iron

32] Portion of the hammer used for fixing the handle is...

A] Face

B] Peen
C] Cheek
D] Eye hole
33] Weight of the hammer for the marking purpose is...
A] 250g
B] 500g
C] 1 kg
D] 2 kgs

Hammer

34] The size of the dividers are specified by the...
A] Total length of the legs
B] Distance between the points when fully opened
C] Length of legs without the points
D] Distance between the pivot and the point
35] The included angle of the groove of 'V' block is always....
A] 45°
B] 60°
C] 90°
D] 120°
36] 'V' blocks are available in grades of...
A] A & B
B] A,B & C
C] 1,2 & 3
D] 1 & 2
37] 'V' blocks of grade 'B' are made of
A] Cast iron
B] Mild steel
C] Steel

D] Cast steel

38] Name the punch used to locate the centre.

A] Prick punch 30°

B] Prick punch 60°

C] Centre punch

D] Dot punch

Centre punch

39] The point angle of centre punch is --------

A] 30°

B] 50°

c] 900

D] 1200

40] Punches are used for forming ---------of any shape

A] Holes

B] Mining

C] Knurling

D] Reaming

41] Generally the length of the handle of the vice is ----------

A] 1.5 times the normal size of the vice

B] 2.5 times the normal size of the vice

C] 3.5 times the normal size of the vice

D] 4.5 times the normal size of the vice

Bench vice

42] Bench vice spindle is made of ....

A] mild steel

B] Cast iron

C] Tool steel

D] Bronze

43] The convexity of files helps...

A] To file concave surfaces

B] To file convex surfaces

C] To prevent rounding of edges of work

D] The file to become straight when pressure is applied

Files

44] Which file used for filling wood, leather and other soft material? .

A] Single cut file

B] Double cut file

c] Rasp cut file

D] Curved cut file

45] File used is used for ------------

A] Cleaning the work piece

C] Renewing the file teeth

B] cleaning the file teeth

D] Cleaning the chips

46] File card is used to --------

A] Clean the work piece

C] Renew the file teeth

B] Clean the file teeth

47] The point angle of scriber is -----------

A] 30°

B] 60°

C] 5° to 10°

D] 12° to 15°

48] The cutting angle for chipping cast iron is...

A] 37.5°

B] 55°

C] 60°

D] 90°

49] The chisel will dig into the material when...

A] The rake angle is more

B] The clearance angle is too low

C] The angle of inclination is more

D] The angle of inclination is too low

50] A slight convexity is given to the cutting edge to...

A] Cut curved surfaces

B] Cut sharp corners

C] Prevent digging of the ends

D] Allow the lubricant to enter

51] Surface plates are made of...

A] High grade cast steel

B] Fine-grained cast iron

C] Alloy steels

D] Wrought iron

52] Surface plates are specified by their length and breadth & are in
A] decimetre
B] Cubic meter
C] Cylindrical
53] Ribs are given on the unmachined portion of the angle plate for...
A] Easy handling
B] Convenience in manufacturing
C] Clamping while setting on machines
D] Rigidity and to prevent distortion
54] The slots on the angle plate are given for...
A] Reducing weight
B] Aligning the work
C] Lifting using hooks
D] Accommodating bolts.
55] The size of the angle plates is stated by...
A] Weight
B] Length
C] Length x width
D] Size number
56] for high speed parting off work on material like cemented carbide Is‘
A] Do all machine
B] Cutting off machine
C] Heavy duty power saw
D] Mining machine sitting saw
57] Gun metal is an alloy of copper, ------------
A] tin and zinc
B] Lead and zinc
C] Zinc and nickel
D] Lead and nickel
58] Cast iron is used for manufacturing machine beds because -------

A] it can resist more compressive stress

B] it is heavy in weight

C] It is cheaper metal

D] It is a brittle metal

59] Accuracy or least count of a metric outside micrometric is ---------

A] 0-1 mm

B] 0.01 mm

C] 0.001 mm

D] 0.02 mm

60] 1000 microns means -----

A] 1 mm

B] 1 m

C] 1000 mm

D] 10 cm

61] in a metric micrometer, a complete revolution of thimble advances -----------

A] 0.01 mm

B] 0.25 mm

C] 0.50 mm

D] 1.00mm

Micrometer

62] Ratchet Stop in the micrometer helps to ------------

A] Control the pressure

B] lock the spindle

C] Adjust the zero error

D] Hold the work piece

63] 1000 micron means ------------

A] 1 mm

B] 1 m

C] 1000 mm

D] 10 cm

64] What is the zero reading of a 50-75 mm outside micrometer?

A] 0.000 mm

B] 0.01 mm

C] 25.00 mm

D] 50.00 mm

65] The value of the smallest division on sleeve of a metric outside micrometer is -----

A] 0.50 mm

B] 1.00 mm

C] 1.50 mm

D] 2.00 mm

66] Ratchet stop in the micrometer helps to ---------

A] control the pressure

B] Lock the spindle

C] Adjust the zero error

D] Hold the work piece

67] Least count of depth micrometer is

A] 0.5 mm

B] 0.2 mm

C] 0.001 mm

D] 0.01 mm

Depth micrometer

68] The least count of vernier calliper is (main scale = 49 division, vernier scale = 50 division]

A] 0.1 mm

B] 0.01 mm

C] 0.001 mm

D] 0.02 mm

Vernier Calliper

69] The type of measurement made by using a Vernier Calliper is -------

A] Direct measurement

B] Indirect measurement

C] 90“] (a] 81 (b]

D] None of these

70] The least count of a vernier bevel protractor is...

A] 1”

B] 5’

C] 1◦

D] 5 ◦

71] The part of a vernier bevel protractor which is normally used as a reference base for measuring angles is the...

A] Blade

B] Stock

C] Disc

C] Main scale

Vernier bevel protractor

72] The part of a vernier bevel protector on which main scale divisions are marked is the...

A] Stock

B] Dial

C] Disc

D] Adjustable blade

73] The part of a bevel protractor, which comes in contact with the inclined surface while measuring is the...

A] Blade

B] Stock

C] Disc

D] Dial

74] The value of each division of the main scale of a vernier bevel protractor is...

A] 5'

B] 1°

C] 5°

D]10°

75] The value of each division of the vernier scale of a bevel protractor is...

A] 1°

B] 1◦5’

C] 1◦55’

D] 5’

76] The taper shank drills are held on the machine by means of...

A] Chucks

B] Sleeves

C] Drift

D] Vice

77] Drill chucks are fitted on the drilling machine spindle by means of a...

A] Knurled ring

B] Arbor

C] Drift

D] Pinion and key

78] The Morse taper provided on drills ranges between...

A] MT 1 to MT 5

B] MT 1 to MT 4

C] MT 0 to MT 5

D] MT 0 to MT 4

79] A drift is used for...

A] Drawing a drill location

B] Fixing chuck on the machine spindle

C] Removing a broken drill from the work

D] Removing the drill from the machine spindle

80] When the taper shank of the drill is larger than the machine spindle, the device to hold the drill is a...

A] Drill sleeve

B] Taper socket

C] Drill drift

D] Chuck and key

81] The suitable cutting fluid for drilling mild steel in a drilling machine is...

A] Synthetic soluble oil
B] Neat oil
C] Distilled water
D] Soluble oil
82] A special feature of the radial drilling machine is...
A] It can be used for drilling with a H.S.S. drill
B] Table can be moved and set at any position
C] A variety of speeds is available
D] The spindle can be brought to any position

83] The point angle of drills depends on...
A] The size of the drill
B] The type of machine
C] The material of the work
D] The RPM of the drill
84] The point angle for a standard drill is...
A] 60°
B] 108°
C] 118°
D] 135°
85] The helical angle determines the...
A] Cutting angle
B] Chew angle
C] Rake angle
D] Lip angle
86] The clearance angle of the drill is between...
A] 3° to 5°
B] 8° to 12°

C] 12◦ to 20◦

D] 15◦ to 20◦

87] In a remote place (no electricity available] a rail track is to be drilled. Choose the right drilling machine

A] Radial drilling machine

B] Pillar drilling machine

C] Ratchet drilling machine

D] Sensitive drilling Machine

Drilling

88] A drilling machine used by a carpenter for cabinet making is a...

A] Ratchet drilling machine

B] Radial drilling machine

C] Breast drilling machine

D] Sensitive drilling machine

89] Which one of the following drilling machines is used for drilling holes where electricity is not available?

A] Bench drilling machine

B] Pillar drilling machine

C] Redial drilling machine

D] Ratchet drilling machine

90] Which one of the following drilling machine is used for heavy duty work?

A] Bench drilling machine

B] Pillar drilling machine

C] Radial drilling machine

D] Electric hand drilling machine

91] Drill chuck are held on the machine spindle by means of ------

A] arbor

B] Drift

C] draw-in bar

D] Chuck nut

92] Different speeds are obtained in a sensitive bench drilling machine by ----

A] Belt pulley mechanism

B] Hydraulic mechanism

C] Rack and Pinion mechanism

D] Cam and follower mechanism

93] The process of heating and cooling to change the structure of steel for obtaining the required properties is called

A] Hardening

B] Normalizing

C] Heat treatment

D] Tempering

94] The main purpose of annealing is to

A] Increase the hardness

B] Increase the toughness

C] Improve machinability

D] Improve distortion

95] The purpose of normalizing steel is to -----------

A] Remove the induced Stress

B] Improve genes and reduce brittleness

C] Soften the metal

D] Increase the surface?

96] Which one of the following process is used for hardenmg the outer 5” Annealing

A] Hardening

B] Tempering

C] Case Hardening

D] Tear surface

97] The purpose of producmg a component with tough and ductIle core and hard ou is known as......

A] Hardening

B] Case hardening

C] Tempering

D] annealing

98] Lower critical temperature of high carbon steel while hardening is ----------

A] 9600C

B] 900°C

c] 7230 c

D] 56O C

99] The process of Changing the structure and thus changing the properties by heating and 'cooling is known as

A] Heat treatment

B] Alloying

C] Tempering

D] None of these

100] For refining the grain structure which one of the following heat treatment processes 'Is adopted.

A] Annealing

B] Hardening

C] Tempering

D] Normalising

101] Annealing is performed on iron and steel ---------

A] To remove internal stresses

B] To reduce hardness

C] To improve machinability

D] All of these

102] Which one of the following does not fall under the stages of heat treatment?

A] Heating

B] Cleaning

C] Quenching

D] Soaking

20] METAL 02

103] Gun metal is an alloy of copper, ------------

A] tin and zinc

B] Lead and zinc

C] Zinc and nickel

D] Lead and nickel

104] for making gutters, roof flashing, hoods etc.

A] Galvanised iron

B] Stainless steel

C] Copper sheet

D] Metal sheets

105] in dairies. food processing, kitchen ware etc.

A] Galvanised iron

B] Stainless steel

C] Copper sheet

D] Metal sheets

106] for making buckets, heating ducts, cabinets etc.

A] Galvanised iron

B] Stainless steel

C] Copper sheet

D] Metal sheets

107] Punching a number of holes in a sheet is known as?

a) Perforating

b) Parting

c) Notching

d) Lancing

108] Shearing the sheet into two or more pieces is known as?

a) Perforating

b) Parting

c) Notching

d) Lancing

109] Removing the pieces from the edge in shearing operation is known as?

a) Perforating

b) Parting

c) Notching

d) Lancing

110] Leaving a tab without removing any material is known as?

a) Perforating

b) Parting

c) Notching

d) Lancing

111] Moving a small straight punch up and down rapidly into a die is done by a process known as?

a) Perforating

b) Parting

c) Nibbling

d) Lancing

112] As the thickness of sheet is increased the clearance needed will also?

a) Increase

b) Decrease

c) No effect

d) First decrease then increase

113] Bevelling is particularly suitable for shearing of?

a) Thin blanks

b) Thick blanks

c) Very thin blanks

d) None of the Mentioned

114] Which of the following is a type of die?

a) Simple dies

b) Progressive dies

c) Compound die

d) All of the Mentioned

115] Which of the following die can perform multiple operations such as blanking, punching, notching etc.?

a) Simple dies

b) Progressive dies

c) Compound die

d) None of the Mentioned

116] As the clearance increases, the punch force required?

a) Decreases

b) Increases

c) Remains same

d) First increases then decrease

117] Maximum temperature for forging H. S. S. is ------------degree.

A] 1200

B] 100

C] 1100

D] 1500

118] Main purpose Of annealing is ----------.

A] to improve machinability

B] to improve magnetism

C] to increase hardness

D] to increase toughness

119] The carbon percentage in H.S.S. tool is -------

A] 0.75 to 1.00 %

B] 1.00 to 2.00 00

C] 0.60 to 0.75 %

D] 0.02 to 0.03 %.

120] Which one of the following is the resistance of a metal to elastic deformation?

A] Ductility.

B] Strength

C] Stiffness

D] Toughness

121] in canneries and chemical plants Metal sheets

A] Galvanised iron

B] Stainless steel

C] Copper sheet

D] Metal sheets

122] Alloy steel, good corrosive resistance and welds easily

A] Black iron

B] Galvanised iron

C] Stainless steel

D] Aluminium

123] Cheapest, can be rolled to any desired thickness

A] Black iron

B] Galvanised iron

C] Stainless steel

D] Aluminium

124] Resists against rust bright silvery appearance

A] Black iron

B] Galvanised iron

C] Stainless steel

D] Aluminium

125] Corrodes rapidly. Bluish black appearance

A] Black iron

B] Galvanised iron

C] Stainless steel

D] Aluminium

126] Drill a blind hole equal to half of the diameter of the stud. Insert this tool into the hole and remove the stud by turning this anticlockwise.

A] Prick Punch Method

B] Filing square very mm

C] Using square taper punch

D] Ezy-out method

127] If the stud is broken near to the surface, employ this method to remove the stud.

A] Prick Punch Method

B] Filing square very mm

C] Using square taper punch

D] Ezy-out method

128] When a stud is broken a little above the surface this method is used to remove the stud.

A] Filing square very mm

B] Using square taper punch

C] Ezy-out method

D] Making drill hole

129] To extract the broken stud a special tool is employed in this method.

A] Prick Punch Method

B] Filing square very mm

C] Using square taper punch

D] Ezy-out method

130] File the protruding stud into square form and remove it.

A] Prick Punch Method

B] Filing square very mm

C] Using square taper punch

D] Ezy-out method

131] Ammonium chloride is used as a flux for soldering...

A] steel

B] aluminium

C] galvanized iron

D] stainless steel

132] Soldering of M.S sheets takes place at a temperature of...

A] $150^{\circ}C$

B] $250^{\circ}C$

C] $400^{\circ}C$

D] $850^{\circ}C$

133.] In soldering operation the base metal is...

A.] not heated

B.] heated to 200◦C

C.] heated to 650◦C

D.] heated to red hot condition

134] Rivets for Joining sheets to thick plates.

A] Countersunk head

B] Flat head

C] Pan head

D] Mushroom

135] Rivets for Joining sheet metal.

A] Countersunk head

B] Flat head

C] Pan head

D] Mushroom

136] Rivets for Heavy fabrication work.

A] Countersunk head

B] Flat head

C] Pan head

D] Mushroom

137] Rivets for Reduces the height of rivet head above the meta\ surface

A] Countersunk head

B] Flat head

C] Pan head

D] Mushroom

138] Rivets for commonly used for structural work.

A] Countersunk head

B] Flat head

C] Pan head

D] Snap head

139] The pressure of acetylene gas for gas cutting a 10mm M.S plate is...

A.] 0.15 kgf/cm2

B.] 0.5 kgf/cm2

C.] 1.0 kgf/cm2

D.] 1.5 kgf/cm2

140] What size of the cutting nozzle you will select for cutting 10mm thick mild steel?

A.] 0.8 mm

B.] 1.2 mm

C.] 1.6 mm

D.] 2.0 mm

141] The angle of filler rod in case of rightward welding technique is...

A.] 10 to 20°

B.] 20 to 30°

C.] 30 to 40°

D.] 40 to 50°

142] One of the advantages of the high pressure system of gas welding is...

A.] it is cheaper

B.] it is portable

C.] it is less dangerous

D.] it does not require a skilled welder

143] The function of a gas regulator is...

A.] get different types of flames

B.] mix the gases in the required proportion

C.] change the volume of gas flowing to the blow pipe

D.] set the working pressure

144] For welding a lap fillet joint in vertical position by gas what should be the angle of below pipe to the line of weld?

A.] 30◦ to 40◦

B.] 45◦to 50◦

C.] 60◦ to 70◦

D.] 75◦ to 80◦

145] Which metal pipe should NOT be used for passing acetylene gas in order to avoid explosions?

A.] galvanized iron

B.] stainless steel

C.] mild steel

D.] cooper

146] he percentage of carbon in acetylene gas is...

A.] 99%

B.] 92.3%

C.] 89.1%

D.] 85.3%

147] Acetylene gas contains

A.] calcium, carbon and hydrogen

B.] calcium and hydrogen

C.] calcium, carbon, hydrogen and oxygen

D.] carbon and hydrogen

148] In an acetylene purifier the sulphureted and phosphorated hydrogen are removed by...

A.] pumice

B.] water

C.] filter wool

D.] purifying chemicals

149] One of the functions of flux in gas welding is...

A.] dissolve the metal oxides

B.] reduce the melting point of mental

C.] increase the flame temperature

D.] increase the root penetration

150] On which of the following factors, the choice of flux for gas welding depend?

A.] type of material to be joined

B.] type of edge penetration

C.] type of fuel gas

D.] type of flame used

151] The divergence allowance required for gas welding a 300mm long copper butt joint is...

A.] 1 to 2 mm

B.] 2 to 3 mm

C.] 3 to 4 mm

D.] 4 to 5 mm

152] The type of edge preparation done for gas welding a 4mm thick copper butt joint is...

A.] single bevel

B.] single V

C.] double V

D.] square

153] The size of nozzle used to gas weld 3.15 mm thick aluminium butt joint is...

A.] 13
B.] 10
C.] 7
D.] 5

154] What is the value of preheating temperature for gas welding of aluminium?

A.] 100 to 120◦C
B.] 150 to 180◦C
C.] 180 to 200◦C
D.] 210 to 250◦C

155] Name the tool used to make and finish the leak proof joints of a pipe T joint

A.] groover
B.] setting hammer
C.] creasing hammer
D.] round bottom stake

156] The angle of vee groove of a single vee but joint for cast iron welding is...

A.] 60◦
B.] 70◦
C.] 80◦
D.] 90◦

157] Shielded metal arc welding is classified under the process of...

A.] electric resistance welding
B.] special welding
C.] electric arc welding
D.] electro gas welding

158] How to specify the size of an electrode holder?

A.] by its weight
B.] by its shape
C.] by its current carrying capacity
D.] by the metal used for making it

159] The current set for a 3.15mm medium coated mild steel electrode is...

A.] 50 to 80 amp
B.] 90 to 120 amp
C.] 120 to 150 amp

D.] 150 to 170 amp

160] A long arc is used in...

A.] welding with a low hydrogen electrode

B.] horizontal position

C.] plug or slot welding

D.] cast iron welding

161] If the travel speed of electrode is high, which type of weld defect you will get on a T fillet joint?

A.] overlap

B.] slag inclusion

C.] excessive reinforcement

D.] lack of root penetration

162] Which weld defect occurs on a lap fillet joint due to improper weaving of the electrode in the covering/final run?

A.] crack

B.] undercut

C.] lack of fusion

D.] edge of plate melted off

163] Which one of the following is used in the oxy-arc cutting process?

A.] flux coated solid electrode

B.] bare wire tubular electrode

C.] flux coated tubular electrode

D.] bare tungsten arc cutting electrode

164] The electrode holder in a carbon arc cutting equipment is made up of...

A.] plain carbon steel

B.] galvanized iron

C.] aluminium

D.] copper

165] The taper shank drills are held on the machine by means of...

A. Chucks

B. Sleeves

C. Drift

D. Vice

166] Drill chucks are fitted on the drilling machine spindle by means of a...

A.] Knurled ring

B.] Arbor

C.] Drift

D.] Pinion and key

167] The Morse taper provided on drills ranges between...

A.] MT 1 to MT 5

B.] MT 1 to MT 4

C.] MT 0 to MT 5

D.] MT 0 to MT 4

168] A drift is used for...

A.] Drawing a drill location

B.] Fixing chuck on the machine spindle

C.] Removing a broken drill from the work

D.] Removing the drill from the machine spindle

169] When the taper shank of the drill is larger than the machine spindle, the device to hold the drill is a...

A.] Drill sleeve

B.] Taper socket

C.] Drill drift

D.] Chuck and key

170] The process of enlarging the end of a hole for accommodating the socket screw head is...

A.] Reaming

B.] Spot facing

C.] Counter boring

D.] Counter sinking

171] Appropriate tool used for spot facing operation is...

A.] Reamer

B.] Counter sinks

C.] Fly cutters

D.] Lathe tool

172] Centre drilling is an operation of...

A.] Drilling and countersinking

B.] Drilling and counter boring

C.] Marking the centre location before drilling

D.] Enlarging the diameter of a hole

173] A short reamer with an axial hole used with an arbor or mandrel is called -------

A] Parallel reamer

B] Adjustable reamer

C] Expansion reamer

D] Chucking reamer

Reamer

174] Which one of the following machine reamers is used to correct the misalignment between the reamer axis and the work axis?

A] Floating blade reamer

B] Machine jig reamer.

C] Shell reamer

D] Chucking reamer

175] Tap are re sharpened by grinding -----

A] Hutes

B] Threads

C] Diameter

D] Relief

176] 50 metric coarse thread is designated as M12 x 125 What does ‘12‘ indicate?

A] Major diameter

B] Root diameter

C] Pitch diameter

D] Blank diameter

177] find the change gears required to cut a 3 mm pitch on 3 lat ’ mm pitch 120

A] Driver / Driven =.455/120

B] Driver/ Driven = 60/120

C] Driver / Driven = 80/120

D] Driver/ Driven 2 40/80 of 5 mm

178] calculate the gears required to cut a 1 5 mm pitch on a lathe havmg lead screw Pitch

A] Driver / Driven -_20/100

B] Driver/ Driven = 30/100

C] Driver / Driven = 40/120

D] Driver/ Driven = 60/120

179] the top surface joining the two sides of adjacent thread is called

A] Crest

B] Root

C] Flank

D] Thread is angle

Thread

180] The included angle of the ISO metric thread is --------

A] 27 1 /2°

B] 30°

C] 55°

D] 60°

181] Which one of the following screw thread forms has an included angle of 55° between the flanks of threads?

A] B. A. Thread

B] Acme thread

C] Buttress threads

D] Knuckle thread

182] Which one of the following is used only for finishing and maintaining correct form of thread?

A] Tap

B] Threading tool

C] Threading chaser

D] Tipped tool

183] The angle Of IS thread (V shaped] is ----------

A] 29°

B] 47 1/4°

C] 50°

D] 60

184] In which of the following methods, only external threads are made -------

A] Form tool mEthOd

B] Compound rest method

C] Tailstock offset method

D] Taper turning attachment method.

185] The surface joining the crest and the root of a thread is known as ----

A] Flank

B] Shank

C] Pitch surface

D] All Of these

186] Pitch of a two start thread is 4 mm. Then the lead of the thread is given by -----

A] 4mm

B] 2mm

C] 8mm

D] 6mm

187] The Gear ratio required for cutting a screw thread of 2.5 mm on a lathe having a lead screw pitch using single point cutting tool is ----

A] 1:2

B] 2:1

C] 1:1 mm

188] A die in which more than one cutting operation is per formed in one stroke

A] Piercing die

B] Progressive die

C] Combination die

D] Compound die

189] A die in which cutting and non cutting operations are carried out per stroke.

A] Piercing die

B] Progressive die

C] Combination die

D] Compound die

Tap Die

190] A die in which two or more sequential operations are performed at two or more stations upon the work.

A] Piercing die

B] <u>Progressive die</u>

C] Combination die

D] Compound die

191] A die in which the shape of the punch and die are directly reproduced in the metal with little or no metal flow.

A] Progressive die

B] Combination die

C] Compound die

D] <u>Forming die</u>

192] The die used for producing any shape of holes.

A] <u>Piercing die</u>

B] Progressive die

C] Combination die

D] Compound die

193] Abrasives are classifications into............

<u>A] Two types</u>

B] Three types

c] One types

D] Four types

194] Grinding wheels made out of---------------- abrasive are most common because of its free and cool cutting action.

<u>A] Aluminium oxide</u>

B] Silicon oxide

C] Ammonium oxide

D] Carbide.

195] Which among the following abrasive is mostly used for cutting off wheels for cutting non metallic materials?

A] Aluminium oxide

<u>B] Silicon carbide</u>

C] Diamond

D] None of above

196] Which abrasive particle is used for grinding tungsten carbide tool insert?

<u>A] Silicon carbide</u>

B] A|203

C] Diamond

D] Corundum

197] Which of the following is the natural abrasive?

A] Aluminium oxide

B] Silicon

C] Boron carbide

<u>D] Corundum</u>

198] Which of the following is the manufactured abrasive?

A] Corundum.

B] Quartz

<u>C] Silicon</u>

D] Emery

199] Which abrasive particle is used for grinding steel fittings?

A] Silicon carbide

<u>B] Aluminium oxide</u>

C] Diamond.

D] boron oxide

200] What kind of abrasive cut of wheel should be used to cut concrete stone and masonry?

A] Silicon

B] Al203

<u>C] Diamond grit</u>

D] Glass

201] Aluminium oxide wheel is used for grinding ------------

A] cast iron

B] Cemented carbide.

<u>C] HSS ‘</u>

D] ceramic

202] The bond of diamond wheel suitable for offhand grinding of the tipped tool is ....

A] Resinoid

B] Vitrified

C] Shellac

D] Metal

Grinding Wheel

203] Which among the following bonds, is used commonly?

A] Vitrified bond '

B] Rubber bond

C] Shellac bond

D] Silicate bond

204] The symbol conventionally used for resinoid .bond is ~~~~~~~~

A] v

B] R f

C] B

D] E

205] In grinding practice the term "grade of wheel" refers to ---------'

A] Hardness of the abrasive used

B] Strength of the bond of the wheel

C] Finish 0f the Wheel

D] Hardness of the work pieces

206] Which bond is used in cut of wheels?

A] Rubber

B] Vitrified

C] Resirjoid

D] Shellac

207] Hardness of grinding wheel is determine by ----------

A] the resistance exerted. by the bond against grinding Stress

B] Hardness of abrasive grains

C] Hardness of bond

D] Ability to penetration

208] When it is required to run a Grinding wheel safely at very high speed, which bond should be used? "

A] Vitrified

B] Shellac

C] Silicate

D] resinoid‘ and rubber

209] in surface grinding what is the suitable range of grain size of the grinding wheel for general purpose surface grinding?

A] 20 to 36

B] 46 to 60

C] 80 to 120

D] 150 to 300

210] AS per Indian Standard, the grain ’46’.comes under the group of «w. -----

A] Coarse

B] Medium

C] Fine

D] Very fine

211] The grit size of the abrasives used in the grinding wheel is usually specified by ----------

A] Hardness number

B] A size of wheel

C] Softness or hardness of the abrasive

D] Mesh number

212] Bench grinder are used for ....

A] Heavy duty work

B] Heavy and light duty work

C] Light duty work

D] Lather work

213] Bench Grinders are fitted on a ....

A] Base

B] Table.

C] Wheel guards

D] Conveyor

225] Which one of the following is important factor required to achieve the interchange ability in mass production? .

A] Geometrical accuracy.

B] Standardization

C] Dimensional accuracy

D] Surface finish

226] Interchange ability is normally applied for? _

A] Repairing of parts

B] Mass production

C] Single piece production

D] All of these

227] When tolerance given in one side of the basic dimension, it is called --------

A].Tolerance system

B] Unilateral tolerance

C] Bilateral tolerance

D] Allowance System

228] The measured Size Of the dimensions of a component as called---------

A] Basic size

B] Nominal Size

C] Allowed size

D] Actual size

229] In the drawing the dimensions of a shaft is shown 40i 0068/0042, which is the size of Shaft within the tolerance?

A] 4.0.64 mm

B] 40.042 mm

C] 40.000 mm

D] 39.998 mm

230] In Hole basic system ----------

A] The size of the shaft is made constant

B] The Size of the hole is made constant

C] Only 'allowance is given on the hole

D] The permissible tolerance are given on the hole and the Shaft

231] The Size of a component is given as 24 -0.1. What does -O.1 indicates? _

A] Upper deviation is + 0.1 mm .

B] Lower deviation is 0.0 mm

C] Fundamental deviation is 0.0 mm

D] Lower deviation is _0.1 mm

232] The tolerance of a hole iS the difference between the -------

A] Maximum hole Size and maximum Shaft size

B] Maximum hole size and maximum hole Size

C] Minimum'hole size and maximum Shaft Size

D] Minimum hole Size and minimum shaft Size

233] A hole whose lower deviation is zero is called basic hole. Which one of the following letter indicates basic hole?

A] E

B] F

C] G '

D] H

234] Which one having upper deviation zero?

A] Bassc Shaft

B] Basic hole

C] Tolerance

D] Clearance

235] A ball bearing on a shaft is type of fit? ,

A] Clearance fit

B] Driving fit

C] Shrinkage fit

D] None of the above

236] In the BIS system of limits and fits, the grade of tolerance are represented by number Symbols and there are ---------i

A] 14 grades of tolerance

B] 16 grades of tolerance

C] 18 grades of tolerance '

D] 20 grades of tolerance

237] A Product is said to have the quality when ....

Limit fit tolerance

A] Its shape and dimensions are within the

B] It is fit for use

C] It appears to be very good

D] The choice of material is right

238] The maximum clearance required between hole'30 +0.021, 0.000 and shaft 30 -0.110, 0.143 is.

A] 0.110 mm '

B]0.131 mm

C] 0.164 mm

D] 0.143 mm

239] A dimension is stated as 25 .1002 mm in a drawing. What is the tolerance?

A] +0.02 mm'

B] +0.04 mm

C] -0.02 mm

D] 25.00 mm

240] A pin is fitted in a hole. The tolerance zone of the pin is entirely above that of hole. The fit obtained will be?

A] Clearance fit

B] Transition fit

C] Interference fit

D] Running fit

241] Tolerance is given to the part size to............

A] Production the part within the required permissible size error

B] Increase the production

C] Decrease the Production

D] Finish the components approximately

242] Which one of the following is the clearance fit under the whole basic system?

A] 20 H7/p6'

B] 2067/211

C] ZOG/gll .

D] 20H/g11.

243] The three classes of fits as per BIS system aré ....

A] Clearance fit, interference fit and transition fit

B] Medium fit, push fit and tight fit

C] Flat fit, round fit and square fit

D] 'Sliding fit ', loose fit and shrinkage fit

244] Which one of the following tolerance specifications has a maximum dimensionless than 20 mm?

A] 20 +0.2,-0.3

B] 20 320.2

C] 20 -0.2, 0.3 e

D]m 20 +500, ~03

245] Difference between the maximum and minimum limit is --------------------

A] Single informant

B] Basic shaft

C] Clearance

D] Tolerance

246] A shaft 55 running freely in bush bearing the type of fit is ---------

A] Clearance fit

B] Driving plate

C] shrinkage fit

D] None of the above

256] -------------is the COFFEC'E dimension when the micrometer measures 45.54mm, if it is having a negative error of 0.02mm

A] 45.58 mm

B] 45 54 mm

C] 45.56 mm

D] 45.53 mm.

257] When the faces of the anvil and the spindle touch each other if the Zero of the Sleeve scale coincides with the zero of the thimble scale, then it is said to be -----------

A] Positive error

B] Negative error

C] Zero error

D] No error

258] Depth bar is used for measurement of -------------

A] Height.

B] Length

C] Depth

D] Inches

259] The dial test indicator shows the measurement as...

A.] The actual size of the component

B.] The difference between the two steps of 5 mm

C.] The magnified small variations in sizes through a pointer

D.] The direct reading of the dimension

260] V -block and dial indicator method is used to measure the

A] Length of the work piece ground

B] Circularity of the surface of the work piece

C] Flatness of the surface

D] Pitch of the thread

261] Which one of the following is not correct about dial test indicator?

A] It has 100 divisions on its dial

B] Motion of the stem is transferred to the dial through Gear train.

C] Its accuracy is 0.1 mm

D] Used in conjunction with depth gauge

317] Threading tools are checked for accuracy for the 60◦ angle by using a

A] Thread plug gauge

B] centre gauge

C] screw pitch gauge

D] tool angle gauge

318] The number of threads per inch can be checked with a

A] tool gauge

B] metric rule by counting

C] ring gauge

D] screw pitch gauge

screw pitch gauge

Sheet Metal MCQ

366] Which method of development is used for developing a rectangular tray?

A] triangular method

B] radial line method

C] parallel line method

D] trial and error method

367] What is the profile of the knife cutting edge of the upper blade of the hand level shear?

A] curved

B] straight

C] inclined

D] beveled

368] For what purpose a groover is used in sheet metal work?

A] to make a hem

B] to make grooves

C] to close and lock the seams

D] to strength then the edge of a job

369] Which type of stake is to be selected for making sharp bends, folding of edges of sheet metal?

A] hatchet stake

B] beak iron stake

C] square edge stake

D] tinman's anvil stake

370] Ammonium chloride is used as a flux for soldering...

A] steel

B] aluminium

C] galvanized iron

D] stainless steel

371] Name the tool used to make and finish the leak proof joints of a pipe T joint

A] groover

B] setting hammer

C] creasing hammer

D] round bottom stake

372] Which one of the following metals will not permit X-rays to pass through?

A] stainless steel

B] aluminium

C] lead

D] tin

373] The frequency of up and down vibration of the cutting edge in a nibbling machine is...

A] 1000 to 1500 times

B] 1500 to 2500 times

C] 2800 to 3000 times

D] 3000 to 3500 times

374] Name the instrument used to check the perpendicularity of the branch pipe with the main pipe of a pipe T joint

A] protractor

B] try square

C] spirit level

D] straight edge

375].Which type of notch is used when a single hem meets at right angles?

A] V notch

B] slit notch

C] slant notch

D] square notch

376] To cut out small apertures which punch and die type of machine is used?

A] shear type nibbler

B] punch type nibbler

C] circular cutting machine

D] guillotine shearing machine

377] The overheating of the blow pipe nozzle is to be avoided because it will

A] cause back fire

B] consume more oxygen and acetylene

C] create burn through defect in the joint

D] create undercut defect in the joint

378] State the nozzle size you will select to weld a 3.15mm thick mild steel sheet

A] 3

B.5

C] 7

D] 10

379] The type of flame to be set for welding brass is...

A] air acetylene flame

B] neutral flame

C] oxidizing flame

D] carburizing flame

380] What is the maximum thickness of mild steel sheet recommended for gas welding using leftward technique?

A] 12mm

B] 10mm

C] 8mm

D] 5mm

381].The distance between the root and toe of a fillet weld is called...

A] root gap

B] leg length

C] reinforcement

D] throat thickness

382] Name the weld defect which occurs due to improper cleaning of the mild steel sheet edge and surface

A] lack of root penetration

B] burn through

C] undercut

D] porosity

383] Which of the following mechanical properties of metals gives resistance to pulling forces?

A] toughness

B] ductility

C] hardness

D] tensile strength

1. The S.I. unit of power is
(a) Henry
(b) coulomb
(c) <u>watt</u>
(d) watt-hour
2. Electric pressure is also called
(a) resistance
(b) power
(c) <u>voltage</u>
(d) energy
3. The substances which have a large number of free electrons and offer a low
resistance are called
(a) insulators
(b) inductors
(c) semi-conductors
(d) <u>conductors</u>
4. Out of the following which is not a poor conductor ?
(a) Cast iron
(b) <u>Copper</u>
(c) Carbon
(d) Tungsten
5. Out of the following which is an insulating material ?
(a) Copper
(b) Gold
(c) Silver
(d) <u>Paper</u>
6. The property of a conductor due to which it passes current is called
(a) resistance
(b) reluctance
(c) <u>conductance</u>
(d) inductance
7. Conductance is reciprocal of
(a) <u>resistance</u>
(b) inductance
(c) reluctance
(d) capacitance
8. The resistance of a conductor varies inversely as

(a) length
(b) area of cross-section
(c) temperature
(d) resistivity
9. With rise in temperature the resistance of pure metals
(a) increases
(b) decreases
(c) first increases and then decreases
(d) remains constant
10. With rise in temperature the resistance of semi-conductors
(a) decreases
(b) increases
(c) first increases and then decreases
(d) remains constant
11. The resistance of a copper wire 200 m long is 21 Q. If its thickness (diameter)
is 0.44 mm, its specific resistance is around
(a) 1.2 x 10~8 Q-m
(b) 1.4 x 10~8 Q-m
(c) 1.6 x 10""8 Q-m
(d) 1.8 x 10"8 Q-m
13. An instrument which detects electric current is known as
(a) voltmeter
(b) rheostat
(c) wattmeter
(d) galvanometer
14. In a circuit a 33 Q resistor carries a current of 2 A. The voltage across the resistor is
(a) 33 V
(b) 66 v
(c) 80 V
(d) 132 V
15. A light bulb draws 300 mA when the voltage across it is 240 V. The resistance of the light bulb is
(a) 400 Q
(b) 600 Q
(c) 800 Q
(d) 1000 Q

16. The resistance of a parallel circuit consisting of two branches is 12 ohms. If the resistance of one branch is 18 ohms, what is the resistance of the other ?

(a) 18 Q

(b) 36 Q

(c) 48 Q

(d) 64 Q

17. Four wires of same material, the same cross-sectional area and the same length when connected in parallel give a resistance of 0.25 Q. If the same four wires are connected is series the effective resistance will be

(a) 1 Q

(b) 2 Q

(c) 3 Q

(d) 4 Q

18. A current of 16 amperes divides between two branches in parallel of resistances 8 ohms and 12 ohms respectively. The current in each branch is

(a) 6.4 A, 6.9 A

(b) 6.4 A, 9.6 A

(c) 4.6 A, 6.9 A

(d) 4.6 A, 9.6 A

19. Current velocity through a copper conductor is

(a) the same as propagation velocity of electric energy

(b) independent of current strength

(c) of the order of a few ^.s/m

(d) nearly 3 x 108 m/s

20. Which of the following material has nearly zero temperature co-efficient of resistance?

(a) Manganin

(b) Porcelain

(c) Carbon

(d) Copper

21. You have to replace 1500 Q resistor in radio. You have no 1500 Q resistor but have several 1000 Q ones which you would connect

(a) two in parallel

(b) two in parallel and one in series

(c) three in parallel

(d) three in series

22. Two resistors are said to be connected in series when

(a) same current passes in turn through both

(b) both carry the same value of current

(c) total current equals the sum of branch currents

(d) sum of IR drops equals the applied e.m.f.

23. Which of the following statement is true both for a series and a parallel D.C. circuit?

(a) Elements have individual currents

(b) Currents are additive

(c) Voltages are additive

(d) Power are additive

24. Which of the following materials has a negative temperature co-efficient of resistance?

(a) Copper

(b) Aluminum

(c) Carbon

(d) Brass

25. Ohm's law is not applicable to

(a) vacuum tubes

(b) carbon resistors

(c) high voltage circuits

(d) circuits with low current densities

26. Which is the best conductor of electricity ?

(a) Iron

(b) Silver

(c) Copper

(d) Carbon

27. For which of the following 'ampere second' could be the unit ?

(a) Reluctance

(b) Charge

(c) Power

(d) Energy

28. All of the following are equivalent to watt except

(a) (amperes) ohm

(b) joules/sec.

(c) amperes x volts

(d) amperes/volt

29. A resistance having rating 10 ohms, 10 W is likely to be a

(a) metallic resistor

(b) carbon resistor

(c) wire wound resistor

(d) variable resistor

30. Which one of the following does not have negative temperature coefficient ?

(a) Aluminium

(b) Paper

(c) Rubber

(d) Mica

31. Varistors are

(a) insulators

(6) non-linear resistors

(c) carbon resistors

(d) resistors with zero temperature coefficient

32. Insulating materials have the function of

(a) preventing a short circuit between conducting wires

(b) preventing an open circuit between the voltage source and the load

(c) conducting very large currents

(d) storing very high currents

33. The rating of a fuse wire is always expressed in

(a) ampere-hours

(b) ampere-volts

(c) kWh

(d) amperes

34. The minimum charge on an ion is

(a) equal to the atomic number of the atom

(b) equal to the charge of an electron

(c) equal to the charge of the number of electrons in an atom (#) zero

35. In a series circuit with unequal resistances

(a) the highest resistance has the most of the current through it

(b) the lowest resistance has the highest voltage drop

(c) the lowest resistance has the highest current

(d) the highest resistance has the highest voltage drop

36. The filament of an electric bulb is made of

(a) carbon

(b) aluminium

(c) tungsten

(d) nickel

37. A 3 Q resistor having 2 A current will dissipate the power of

(a) 2 watts

(b) 4 watts

(c) 6 watts

(d) 8 watts

38. Which of the following statement is true?

(a) A galvanometer with low resistance in parallel is a voltmeter

(b) A galvanometer with high resistance in parallel is a voltmeter

(c) A galvanometer resistance in series is an ammeter with low

(d) A galvanometer with high resistance in series is an ammeter

39. The resistance of a few meters of wire conductor in closed electrical circuit is

(a) practically zero

(b) low

(c) high

(d) very high

40. If a parallel circuit is opened in the main line, the current

(a) increases in the branch of the lowest resistance

(b) increases in each branch

(c) is zero in all branches

(d) is zero in the highest resistive branch

41. If a wire conductor of 0.2 ohm resistance is doubled in length, its resistance becomes

(a) 0.4 ohm

(b) 0.6 ohm

(c) 0.8 ohm

(d) 1.0 ohm

42. Three 60 W bulbs are in parallel across the 60 V power line. If one bulb burns open

(a) there will be heavy current in the main line

(b) rest of the two bulbs will not light

(c) all three bulbs will light

(d) the other two bulbs will light

43. The four bulbs of 40 W each are connected in series swift a battery across them, which of the following statement is true ?

(a) The current through each bulb in same

(b) The voltage across each bulb is not same

(c) The power dissipation in each bulb is not same

(d) None of the above

44. Two resistances Rl and Ri are connected in series across the voltage source where Rl>Ri. The largest drop will be across

(a) Rl

(b) Ri

(c) either Rl or Ri

(d) none of them

46. A closed switch has a resistance of

(a) zero

(b) about 50 ohms

(c) about 500 ohms

(d) infinity

47. The hot resistance of the bulb's filament is higher than its cold resistance because the temperature co-efficient of the filament is

(a) zero

(b) negative

(c) positive

(d) about 2 ohms per degree

49. The insulation on a current carrying conductor is provided

(a) to prevent leakage of current

(b) to prevent shock

(c) both of above factors

(d) none of above factors

50. The thickness of insulation provided on the conductor depends on

(a) the magnitude of voltage on the conductor

(b) the magnitude of current flowing through it

(c) both (a) and (b)

(d) none of the above

51. Which of the following quantities remain the same in all parts of a series circuit ?

(a) Voltage

(b) Current

(c) Power

(d) Resistance

52. A 40 W bulb is connected in series with a room heater. If now 40 W bulb is replaced by 100 W bulb, the heater output will

(a) decrease

(b) increase

(c) remain same

(d) heater will burn out

53. In an electric kettle water boils in 10 m minutes. It is required to boil the boiler in 15 minutes, using same supply mains

(a) length of heating element should be decreased

(b) length of heating element should be increased

(c) length of heating element has no effect on heating if water

(d) none of the above

54. An electric filament bulb can be worked from

(a) D.C. supply only

(b) A.C. supply only

(c) Battery supply only

(d) All above

55. Resistance of a tungsten lamp as applied voltage increases

(a) decreases

(b) increases

(c) remains same

(d) none of the above

56. Electric current passing through the circuit produces

(a) magnetic effect

(b) luminous effect

(c) thermal effect

(d) chemical effect

(e) all above effects

57. Resistance of a material always decreases if

(a) temperature of material is decreased

(6) temperature of material is increased

(c) number of free electrons available become more

(d) none of the above is correct

58. If the efficiency of a machine is to be high, what should be low ?

(a) Input power

(b) Losses

(c) True component of power

(d) kWh consumed

(e) Ratio of output to input

59. When electric current passes through a metallic conductor, its temperature rises. This is due to

(a) collisions between conduction electrons and atoms

(b) the release of conduction electrons from parent atoms

(c) mutual collisions between metal atoms

(d) mutual collisions between conducting electrons

60. Two bulbs of 500 W and 200 W rated at 250 V will have resistance ratio as

(a) 4 : 25

(b) 25 : 4

(c) 2 : 5

(d) 5 : 2

61. A glass rod when rubbed with silk cloth is charged because

(a) it takes in proton

(b) its atoms are removed

(c) it gives away electrons

(d) it gives away positive charge

62. Whether circuit may be AC. or D.C. one, following is most effective in

reducing the magnitude of the current.

(a) Reactor

(b) Capacitor

(c) Inductor

(d) Resistor

63. It becomes more difficult to remove

(a) any electron from the orbit

(6) first electron from the orbit

(c) second electron from the orbit

(d) third electron from the orbit

64. When one leg of parallel circuit is opened out the total current will

(a) reduce

(b) increase

(c) decrease

(d) become zero

65. In a lamp load when more than one lamp are switched on the total resistance

of the load

(a) increases

(b) decreases

(c) remains same

(d) none of the above

66. Two lamps 100 W and 40 W are connected in series across 230 V (alternating).
Which of the following statement is correct ?
(a) 100 W lamp will glow brighter
(b) 40 W lamp will glow brighter
(c) Both lamps will glow equally bright
(d) 40 W lamp will fuse
67. Resistance of 220 V, 100 W lamp will be
(a) 4.84 Q
(b) 48.4 Q
(c) 484 ft
(d) 4840 Q
68. In the case of direct current
(a) magnitude and direction of current remains constant
(b) magnitude and direction of current changes with time
(c) magnitude of current changes with time
(d) magnitude of current remains constant
69. When electric current passes through a bucket full of water, lot of bubbling is
observed. This suggests that the type of supply is
(a) A.C.
(b) D.C.
(c) any of above two
(d) none of the above
70. Resistance of carbon filament lamp as the applied voltage increases.
(a) increases
(b) decreases
(c) remains same
(d) none of the above
71. Bulbs in street lighting are all connected in
(a) parallel
(b) series
(c) series-parallel
(d) end-to-end
72. For testing appliances, the wattage of test lamp should be
(a) very low
(b) low
(c) high

(d) any value

73. Switching of a lamp in house produces noise in the radio. This is because switching operation produces

(a) arcs across separating contacts

(b) mechanical noise of high intensity

(c) both mechanical noise and arc between contacts

(d) none of the above

74. Sparking occurs when a load is switched off because the circuit has high

(a) resistance

(b) inductance

(c) capacitance

(d) impedance

75. Copper wire of certain length and resistance is drawn out to three times its

length without change in volume, the new resistance of wire becomes

(a) 1/9 times

(b) 3 times

(c) 9 times

(d) unchanged

76. When resistance element of a heater fuses and then we reconnect it after removing a portion of it, the power of the heater will

(a) decrease

(b) increase

(c) remain constant

(d) none of the above

77. A field of force can exist only between

(a) two molecules

(b) two ions

(c) two atoms

(d) two metal particles

78. A substance whose molecules consist of dissimilar atoms is called

(a) semi-conductor

(b) super-conducto

(c) compound

(d) insulator

79. International ohm is defined in terms of the resistance of

(a) a column of mercury

(b) a cube of carbon

(c) a cube of copper

(d) the unit length of wire

80. Three identical resistors are first connected in parallel and then in series.

The resultant resistance of the first combination to the second will be

(a) 9 times

(b) 1/9 times

(c) 1/3 times

(d) 3 times

91. Which method can be used for absolute measurement of resistances ?

(a) Lorentz method

(b) Releigh method

(c) Ohm's law method

(d) Wheatstone bridge method

92. Three 6 ohm resistors are connected to form a triangle. What is the resistance between any two corners ?

(a) 3/2 Q

(b 6 Q

(c) 4 Q

(d) 8/3 Q

93. Ohm's law is not applicable to

(a) semi-conductors

(b) D.C. circuits

(c) small resistors

(d) high currents

94. Two copper conductors have equal length. The cross-sectional area of one conductor is four times that of the other. If the conductor having smaller crosssectional area has a resistance of 40 ohms the resistance of other conductor will be

(a) 160 ohms

(b) 80 ohms

(c) 20 ohms

(d) 10 ohms

95. A nichrome wire used as a heater coil has the resistance of 2 £2/m. For a heater of 1 kW at 200 V, the length of wire required will be

(a) 80 m

(b) 60 m

(c) 40 m

(d) 20 m

96. Temperature co-efficient of resistance is expressed in terms of

(a) ohms/°C

(b) mhos/ohm°C

(c) ohms/ohm°C

98. When current flows through heater coil it glows but supply wiring does not glow because

(a) current through supply line flows at slower speed

(b) supply wiring is covered with insulation layer

(c) resistance of heater coil is more than the supply wires

(d) supply wires are made of superior material

99. The condition for the validity under Ohm's law is that

(a) resistance must be uniform

(b) current should be proportional to the size of the resistance

(c) resistance must be wire wound type

(d) temperature at positive end should be more than the temperature at negative end

100. Which of the following statement is correct ?

(a) A semi-conductor is a material whose conductivity is same as between that of a conductor and an insulator

(b) A semi-conductor is a material which has conductivity having average value of conductivity of metal and insulator

(c) A semi-conductor is one which con¬ducts only half of the applied voltage

(d) A semi-conductor is a material made of alternate layers of conducting material and insulator

101. A rheostat differs from potentiometer in the respect that it

(a) has lower wattage rating

(b) has higher wattage rating

(c) has large number of turns

(d) offers large number of tapping

102. The weight of an aluminium conductor as compared to a copper conductor of identical cross-section, for the same electrical resistance, is

(a) 50%

(b) 60%

(c) 100%

(d) 150%

103. An open resistor, when checked with an ohm-meter reads

(a) zero

(b) infinite

(c) high but within tolerance

(d) low but not zero

104. are the materials having electrical conductivity much less than most of the metals but much greater than that of typical insulators.

(a) Varistors

(b) Thermistor

(c) Semi-conductors

(d) Variable resistors

105. All good conductors have high

(a) conductance

(b) resistance

(c) reluctance

(d) thermal conductivity

106. Voltage dependent resistors are usually made from

(a) charcoal

(b) silicon carbide

(c) nichrome

(d) graphite

107. Voltage dependent resistors are used

(a) for inductive circuits

(b) to supress surges

(c) as heating elements

(d) as current stabilizers

108. The ratio of mass of proton to that of electron is nearly

(a) 1840

(b) 1840

(c) 30

(d) 4

109. The number of electrons in the outer most orbit of carbon atom is

(a) 3

(b) 4

(c) 6

(d) 7

110. With three resistances connected in parallel, if each dissipates 20 W the total power supplied by the voltage source equals

(a) 10 W

(b) 20 W

(c) 40 W

(d) 60 W

111. A thermistor has

(a) positive temperature coefficient

(b) negative temperature coefficient

(c) zero temperature coefficient

(d) variable temperature coefficient

112. If/, R and t are the current, resistance and time respectively, then according

to Joule's law heat produced will be proportional to

(a) I2Rt

(b) I2Rf

(c) I2R2t

(d) I2R2t*

113. Nichrome wire is an alloy of

(a) lead and zinc

(b) chromium and vanadium

(c) nickel and chromium

(d) copper and silver

114. When a voltage of one volt is applied, a circuit allows one micro ampere current to flow through it. The conductance of the circuit is

(a) 1 n-mho

(b) 106 mho

(c) 1 milli-mho

(d) none of the above

115. Which of the following can have negative temperature coefficient ?

(a) Compounds of silver

(6) Liquid metals

(c) Metallic alloys

(d) Electrolytes

116. Conductance : mho ::

(a) resistance : ohm

(b) capacitance : henry

(c) inductance : farad

(d) lumen : steradian

117. 1 angstrom is equal to

(a) 10-8 mm

(b) 10″6 cm

(c) 10″10 m

(d) 10~14 m

118. One newton meter is same as

(a) one watt

(b) one joule

(c) five joules

(d) one joule second

1. "The mass of an ion liberated at an electrode is directly proportional to the quantity of electricity".

The above statement is associated with

(a) Newton's law

(b) Faraday's law of electromagnetic

(c) Faraday's law of electrolysis

(d) Gauss's law

2. The charge required to liberate one gram equivalent of any substance is known as _______ constant

(a) time

(b) Faraday's

(c) Boltzman

3. During the charging of a lead-acid cell

(a) its voltage increases

(b) it gives out energy

(c) its cathode becomes dark chocolate brown in colour

(d) specific gravity of H2SO4 decreases

4. The capacity of a lead-acid cell does not depend on its

(a) temperature

(b) rate of charge

(c) rate of discharge

(d) quantity of active material

5. During charging the specific gravity of the electrolyte of a lead-acid battery

(a) increases

(b) decreases

(c) remains the same

(d) becomes zero

6. The active materials on the positive and negative plates of a fully charged leadacid battery are

(a) lead and lead peroxide

(b) lead sulphate and lead

(c) lead peroxide and lead

(d) none of the above

7. When a lead-acid battery is in fully charged condition, the colour of its positive

plate is

(a) dark grey

(b) brown

(c) dark brown

(d) none of above

8. The active materials of a nickel-iron battery are

(a) nickel hydroxide

(6) powdered iron and its oxide

(c) 21% solution of KOH

(d) all of the above

9. The ratio of ampere-hour efficiency to watt-hour efficiency of a lead-acid cell is

(a) just one

(b) always greater than one

(c) always less than one

(d) none of the above.

10. The best indication about the state of charge on a lead-acid battery is given by

(a) output voltage

(b) temperature of electrolyte

(c) specific gravity of electrolyte

(d) none of the above

11. The storage battery generally used in electric power station is

(a) nickel-cadmium battery

(b) zinc-carbon battery

(c) lead-acid battery

(d) none of the above

12. The output voltage of a charger is

(a) less than the battery voltage

(b) higher than the battery voltage

(c) the same as the battery voltage

(d) none of the above

13. Cells are connected in series in order to

(a) increase the voltage rating

(6) increase the current rating

(c) increase the life of the cells

(d) none of the above

14. Five 2 V cells are connected in parallel. The output voltage is

(a) 1 V

(6) 1.5 V

(c) 1.75 V

(d) 2 V

15. The capacity of a battery is expressed in terms of

(a) current rating

(b) voltage rating

(c) ampere-hour rating

(d) none of the above

16. Duringthe charging and discharging of a nickel-iron cell

(a) corrosive fumes are produced

(b) water is neither formed nor absorbed

(c) nickel hydroxide remains unsplit

(d) its e.m.f. remains constant

17. As compared to constant-current system, the constant-voltage system of charging a lead acid cell has the advantage of

(a) reducing time of charging

(b) increasing cell capacity

(c) both (a) and (b)

(d) avoiding excessive gassing

18. A dead storage battery can be revived by

(a) adding distilled water

(6) adding so-called battery restorer

(c) a dose of H2SO4

(d) none of the above

19. As compared to a lead-acid cell, the efficiency of a nickel-iron cell is less due to its

(a) compactness

(b) lower e.m.f.

(c) small quantity of electrolyte used

(d) higher internal resistance

20. Trickle charging of a storage battery helps to

(a) maintain proper electrolyte level

(b) increase its reserve capacity

(c) prevent sulphation

(d) keep it fresh and fully charged

21. Those substances of the cell which take active part in chemical combination and hence produce electricity during charging or discharging are known as_______materials.

(a) passive

(b) active

(c) redundant

(d) inert

22. In a lead-acid cell dilute sulphuric acid (electrolyte) approximately comprises the following

(a) one part H2O, three parts H2SO4

(b) two parts H2O, two parts H2SO4

(c) three parts H2O, one part H2SO4

(d) all H2S04

23. It is noticed that durum charging

(a) there is a rise in voltage

(b) energy is absorbed by the cell

(c) specific gravity of H2SO4 is increased

(d) all of the above

24. It is noticed that during discharging the following does not happen

(a) both anode and cathode become PbS04

(b) specific gravity of H2SO4 decreases

(c) voltage of the cell decreases

(d) the cell absorbs energy

25. The ampere-hour efficiency of a leadacid cell is normally between

(a) 20 to 30%

(b) 40 to 50%

(c) 60 to 70%

(d) 90 to 95%

26. The watt-hour efficiency of a lead-acid cell varies between

(a) 25 to 35%

(b) 40 to 60%

(c) 70 to 80%

(d) 90 to 95%

27. The capacity of a lead-acid cell is measured in

(a) amperes

(b) ampere-hours

(c) watts

(d) watt-hours

28. The capacity of a lead-acid cell depends on

(a) rate of discharge

(b) temperature

(c) density of electrolyte

(d) all above

29. When the lead-acid cell is fully charged, the electrolyte assumes ______appearance

(a) dull

(b) reddish

(c) bright

(d) milky

30. The e.m.f. of an Edison cell, when fully charged, is nearly

(a) 1.4 V

(b) 1 V

(c) 0.9 V

(d) 0.8 V

31. The internal resistance of an alkali cell is nearly ______ times that of the leadacid cell.

(a) two

(b) three

(c) four

(d) five

32. The average charging voltage for alkali cell is about

(a) 1 V

(b) 1.2 V

(c) 1.7 V

(d) 2.1 V

33. On the average the ampere-hour efficiency of an Edison cell is about

(a) 40%

(b) 60%

(c) 70%

(d) 80%

34. The active material of the positive plates of silver-zinc batteries is

(a) silver oxide

(b) lead oxide

(c) lead

(d) zinc powder

35. Lead-acid cell has a life of nearly charges and discharges

(a) 500

(b) 700

(c) 1000

(d) 1250

36. Life of the Edison cell is at least

(a) five years

(b) seven years

(c) eight years

(d) ten years

37. The internal resistance of a lead-acid cell is that of Edison cell

(a) less than

(b) more than

(c) equal to

(d) none of the above

38. Electrolyte used in an Edison cell is

(a) NaOH

(b) KOH

(c) HC1

(d) HN03

39. Electrolyte used in a lead-acid cell is

(a) NaOH

(b) onlyH2S04

(c) only water

(d) dilute H2SO4

40. Negative plate of an Edison cell is made of

(a) copper

(b) lead

(c) iron

(d) silver oxide

41. The open circuit voltage of any storage cell depends wholly upon

(a) its chemical constituents

(b) on the strength of its electrolyte
(c) its temperature
(d) all above
42. The specific gravity of electrolyte is measured by
(a) manometer
(6) a mechanical gauge
(c) hydrometer
(d) psychrometer
43. When the specific gravity of the electrolyte of a lead-acid cell is reduced to 1.1 to 1.15 the cell is in
(a) charged state
(b) discharged state
(c) both (a) and (b)
(d) active state
44. In ______ system the charging current is intermittently controlled at either a
maximum or minimum value
(a) two rate charge control
(b) trickle charge
(c) floating charge
(d) an equalizing charge
45. Over charging
(a) produces excessive gassing
(b) loosens the active material
(e) increases the temperature resulting in buckling of plates
(d) all above
46. Undercharging
(a) reduces specific gravity of the electrolyte
(b) increases specific gravity of the electrolyte
(c) produces excessive gassing
(d) increases the temperature
47. Internal short circuits are caused by
(a) breakdown of one or more separators
(b) excess accumulation of sediment at the bottom of the cell
(c) both (a) and (b)
(d) none of the above
48. The effect of sulphation is that the internal resistance
(a) increases

(b) decreases

(c) remains same

(d) none of the above

49. Excessive formation of lead sulphate on the surface of the plates happens because of

(a) allowing a battery to stand in discharged condition for a long time

(b) topping up with electrolyte

(c) persistent undercharging

(d) all above

50. The substances which combine together to store electrical energy during the charge are called _______ materials

(a) active

(b) passive

(c) inert

(d) dielectric

1. The property of coil by which a counter e.m.f. is induced in it when the current

through the coil changes is known as

(a) self-inductance

(b) mutual inductance

(c) series aiding inductance

(d) capacitance

2. As per Faraday's laws of electromagnetic induction, an e.m.f. is induced in a

conductor whenever it

(a) lies perpendicular to the magnetic flux

(b) lies in a magnetic field

(c) cuts magnetic flux

(d) moves parallel to the direction of the magnetic field

3. Which of the following circuit element stores energy in the electromagnetic

field ?

(a) Inductance

(b) Condenser

(c) Variable resistor

(d) Resistance

4. The inductance of a coil will increase under all the following conditions except

(a) when more length for the same number of turns is provided

(6) when the number of turns of the coil increase

(c) when more area for each turn is provided

(d) when permeability of the core increases

5. Higher the self-inductance of a coil,

(a) lesser its weber-turns

(b) lower the e.m.f. induced

(c) greater the flux produced by it

(d) longer the delay in establishing steady current through it

6. In an iron cored coil the iron core is removed so that the coil becomes an air cored coil. The inductance of the coil will

(a) increase

(b) decrease

(c) remain the same

(d) initially increase and then decrease

7. An open coil has

(a) zero resistance and inductance

(b) infinite resistance and zero inductance

(c) infinite resistance and normal inductance

(d) zero resistance and high inductance

8. Both the number of turns and the core length of an inductive coil are doubled.

Its self-inductance will be

(a) unaffected

(b) doubled

(c) halved

(d) quadrupled

9. If current in a conductor increases then according to Lenz's law self-induced

voltage will

(a) aid the increasing current

(b) tend to decrease the amount of cur-rent

(c) produce current opposite to the in-creasing current

(d) aid the applied voltage

10. The direction of induced e.m.f. can be found by

(a) Laplace's law

(b) Lenz's law

(c) Fleming's right hand rule

(d) Kirchhoff s voltage law

11. Air-core coils are practically free from

(a) hysteresis losses

(b) eddy current losses

(c) both (a) and (b)

(d) none of the above

12. The magnitude of the induced e.m.f. in a conductor depends on the

(a) flux density of the magnetic field

(b) amount of flux cut

(c) amount of flux linkages

(d) rate of change of flux-linkages

13. Mutually inductance between two magnetically-coupled coils depends on

(a) permeability of the core

(b) the number of their turns

(c) cross-sectional area of their common core

(d) all of the above

14. A laminated iron core has reduced eddy-current losses because

(a) more wire can be used with less D.C. resistance in coil

(b) the laminations are insulated from each other

(c) the magnetic flux is concentrated in the air gap of the core

(d) the laminations are stacked vertfcally

15. The law that the induced e.m.f. and current always oppose the cause producing them is due to

(a) Faraday

(b) Lenz

(c) Newton

16. Which of the following is not a unit of inductance ?

(a) Henry

(b) Coulomb/volt ampere

(c) Volt second per ampere

(d) All of the above

17. In case of an inductance, current is proportional to

(a) voltage across the inductance

(b) magnetic field

(c) both (a) and (b)

(d) neither (a) nor (b)

18. Which of the following circuit elements will oppose the change in circuit

current ?

(a) Capacitance

(b) Inductance

(c) Resistance

(d) All of the above

19. For a purely inductive circuit which of the following is true ?

(a) Apparent power is zero

(b) Relative power is.zero

(c) Actual power of the circuit is zero

(d) Any capacitance even if present in the circuit will not be charged

20. Which of the following is unit of inductance ?

(a) Ohm

(b) Henry

(c) Ampere turns

(d) Webers/metre

21. An e.m.f. of 16 volts is induced in a coil of inductance 4H. The rate of change

of current must be

(a) 64 A/s

(b) 32 A/s

(c) 16 A/s

(d) 4 A/s

22. The core of a coil has a length of 200 mm. The inductance of coil is 6 mH. If

the core length is doubled, all other quantities, remaining the same, the inductance will be

(a) 3 mH

(b) 12 mH

(c) 24mH

(d)48mH

23. The self inductances of two coils are 8 mH and 18 mH. If the co-efficients of

coupling is 0.5, the mutual inductance of the coils is

(a) 4 mH

(b) 5 mH

(c) 6 mH

(d) 12 mH

24. Two coils have inductances of 8 mH and 18 mH and a co-efficient of coupling

of 0.5. If the two coils are connected in series aiding, the total inductance will be

(a) 32 mH

(b) 38 mH

(c) 40 mH

(d) 48 mH

25. A 200 turn coil has an inductance of 12 mH. If the number of turns is

increased to 400 turns, all other quantities (area, length etc.) remaining the same,

the inductance will be

(a) 6 mH

(b) 14 mH

(c) 24 mH

(d) 48 mH

26. Two coils have self-inductances of 10 H and 2 H, the mutual inductance being

zero. If the two coils are connected in series, the total inductance will be

(a) 6 H

(b) 8 H

(c) 12 H

(d) 24 H

27. In case all the flux from the current in coil 1 links with coil 2, the co-efficient

of coupling will be

(a) 2.0

(b) 1.0

(c) 0.5

(d) zero

28. A coil with negligible resistance has 50V across it with 10 mA. The inductive

reactance is

(a) 50 ohms

(b) 500 ohms

(c) 1000 ohms

(d) 5000 ohms

29. A conductor 2 meters long moves at right angles to a magnetic field of flux

density 1 tesla with a velocity of 12.5 m/s. The induced e.m.f. in the conductor will

be

(a) 10 V

(6) 15 V

(c) 25V

(d) 50V

30. Lenz's law is a consequence of the law of conservation of

(a) induced current

(b) charge

(c) energy

(d) induced e.m.f.

31. A conductor carries 125 amperes of current under 60° to a magnetic field of 1.1

tesla. The force on the conductor will be

nearly

(a) 50 N

(b) 120 N

(c) 240 N

(d) 480 N

32. Find the force acting on a conductor 3m long carrying a current of 50 amperes

at right angles to a magnetic field having a flux density of 0.67 tesla.

(a) 100 N

(b) 400 N

(c) 600 N

(d) 1000 N

33. The co-efficient of coupling between two air core coils depends on

(a) self-inductance of two coils only

(b) mutual inductance between two coils only

(c) mutual inductance and self inductance of two coils

(d) none of the above

34. An average voltage of 10 V is induced in a 250 turns solenoid as a result of a

change in flux which occurs in 0.5 second. The total flux change is

(a) 20 Wb
(b) 2 Wb
(c) 0.2 Wb
(d) <u>0.02 Wb</u>

35. A 500 turns solenoid develops an average induced voltage of 60 V. Over what
time interval must a flux change of 0.06 Wb occur to produce such a voltage ?

(a) 0.01 s
(b) 0.1 s
(c) <u>0.5 s</u>
(d) 5 s

36. Which of the fpllowing inductor will have the least eddy current losses ?

(a) <u>Air core</u>
(b) Laminated iron core
(c) Iron core
(d) Powdered iron core

37. A coil induces 350 mV when the current changes at the rate of 1 A/ s. The
value of inductance is

(a) 3500 mH
(b) <u>350 mH</u>
(c) 250 mH
(d) 150 mH

38. Two 300 uH coils in series without mutual coupling have a total inductance of

(a) 300 uH
(b) <u>600 uH</u>
(c) 150 uH
(d) 75 uH

39. Current changing from 8 A to 12 A in one second induced 20 volts in a coil.
The value of inductance is

(a) 5 mH
(b) 10 mH
(c) <u>5 H</u>
(d) 10 H

40. Which circuit element(s) will oppose the change in circuit current ?
(a) Resistance only
(b) Inductance only
(c) Capacitance only
(d) Inductance and capacitance

41. A crack in the magnetic path of an inductor will result in
(a) unchanged inductance
(b) increased inductance
(c) zero inductance
(d) reduced inductance

42. A coil is wound on iron core which carries current I. The self-induced voltage
in the coil is not affected by
(a) variation in coil current
(b) variation in voltage to the coil
(c) change of number of turns of coil
(d) the resistance of magnetic path

1. A semiconductor is formed by .... bonds.
A] Covalent
B] Electrovalent
C] Co-ordinate
D] None of the above

2. A semiconductor has .... temperature coefficient of resistance.
A] Positive
B] Zero
C] Negative
D] None of the above

3. The most commonly used semiconductor is ....
A] Germanium
B] Silicon
C] Carbon
D] Sulphur

6. The resistivity of a pure silicon is about ....
A] 100 O cm
B] 6000 O cm
C] 3 x 105 O m
D] 6 x 10-8 O cm

7. When a pure semiconductor is heated, its resistance ....

A] Goes up

B] Goes down

C] Remains the same

D] Can't say

8. The strength of a semiconductor crystal comes from ....

A] Forces between nuclei

B] Forces between protons

C] Electron-pair bonds

D] None of the above

9. When a pentavalent impurity is added to a pure semiconductor, it becomes ....

A] An insulator

B] An intrinsic semiconductor

C] p-type semiconductor

D] n-type semiconductor

10. Addition of pentavalent impurity to a semiconductor createsmany ....

A] Free electrons

B] Holes

C] Valence electrons

D] Bound electrons

11. A pentavalent impurity has .... Valence electrons

A] 35

B] 4

C] 6

12. An n-type semiconductor is ....

A] Positively charged

B] Negatively charged

C] Electrically neutral

D] None of the above

14. Addition of trivalent impurity to a semiconductor creates many ....

A] Holes

B] Free electrons

C] Valence electrons

D] Bound electrons

15. A hole in a semiconductor is defined as ....

A] A free electron

B] The incomplete part of an electron pair bond

C] A free proton

D] A free neutron

16. The impurity level in an extrinsic semiconductor is about ..... of pure semiconductor.

A] 10 atoms for 108 atoms

B] 1 atom for 108 atoms

C] 1 atom for 104 atoms

D] 1 atom for 100 atoms

17. As the doping to a pure semiconductor increases, the bulk resistance of the semiconductor ....

A] Remains the same

B] Increases

C] Decreases

D] None of the above

18. A hole and electron in close proximity would tend to ....

A] Repel each other

B] Attract each other

C] Have no effect on each other

D] None of the above

19. In a semiconductor, current conduction is due to ....

A] Only holes

B] Only free electrons

C] Holes and free electrons

D] None of the above

20. The random motion of holes and free electrons due to thermal agitation is called ....

A] Diffusion

B] Pressure

C] Ionisation

D] None of the above

21. A forward biased pn junction diode has a resistance of the order of

A] Ok

B] O

C] MO

D] None of the above

22. The battery connections required to forward bias a pn junction are ......

A] +ve terminal to p and –ve terminal to n

B] -ve terminal to p and +ve terminal to n

C] -ve terminal to p and –ve terminal to n

D] None of the above

23. The barrier voltage at a pn junction for germanium is about ....

A] 5 V

B] 3 V

C] Zero

D] <u>3 V</u>

24. In the depletion region of a pn junction, there is a shortage of ....

A] Acceptor ions

B] <u>Holes and electrons</u>

C] Donor ions

D] None of the above

25. A reverse bias pn junction has ....

A] narrow depletion layer

B] <u>Almost no current</u>

C] Very low resistance

D] Large current flow

26. A pn junction acts as a ....

A] Controlled switch

B] Bidirectional switch

C] <u>Unidirectional switch</u>

D] None of the above

27. A reverse biased pn junction has resistance of the order of

A] Ok

B] O

C] <u>MO</u>

D] None of the above

28. The leakage current across a pn junction is due to ....

A] <u>Minority carriers</u>

B] Majority carriers

C] Junction capacitance

D] None of the above

29. When the temperature of an extrinsic semiconductor is increased, the pronounced effect is on......

A] Junction capacitance

B] <u>Minority carriers</u>

C] Majority carriers

D] None of the above

30. With forward bias to a pn junction , the width of depletion layer ....

A] Decreases

B] Increases

C] Remains the same

D] None of the above

31. The leakage current in a pn junction is of the order of

A] Aa

B] mA

C] kA

D] μA

32. In an intrinsic semiconductor, the number of free electrons ....

A] Equals the number of holes

B] Is greater than the number of holes

C] Is less than the number of holes

D] None of the above

33. At room temperature, an intrinsic semiconductor has ....

A] Many holes only

B] A few free electrons and holes

C] Many free electrons only

D] No holes or free electrons

34. At absolute temperature, an intrinsic semiconductor has ....

A] A few free electrons

B] Many holes

C] Many free electrons

D] No holes or free electrons

35. At room temperature, an intrinsic silicon crystal acts approximately as ......

A] A battery

B] A conductor

C] An insulator

D] A piece of copper wire

1. A crystal diode has ....

one pn junction

two pn junctions

three pn junctions

none of the above

ANS: 1

2. A crystal diode has forward resistance of the order of ....
kΩ
Ω
MΩ
none of the above
ANS: 2
3. If the arrow of crystal diode symbol is positive w.r.t. bar, then diode is .... biased.
forward
reverse
either forward or reverse
none of the above
ANS: 1
SEMICONDUCTOR DIODE
Questions and Answers pdf
4. The reverse current in a diode is of the order of ....
kA
mA
μA
A
ANS: 3
5. The forward voltage drop across a silicon diode is about ....
2.5 V
3 V
10 V
0.7 V
ANS: 4
6. A crystal diode is used as ....
an amplifier
a rectifier
an oscillator
a voltage regulator
ANS: 2
7. The d.c. resistance of a crystal diode is .... its a.c. resistance
the same as
more than

less than
none of the above
ANS: 3
8. An ideal crystal diode is one which behaves as a perfect ....
when forward biased.
conductor
insulator
resistance material
none of the above
ANS: 1
9. The ratio of reverse resistance and forward resistance of a
germanium crystal diode is about ....
1 : 1
100 : 1
1000 : 1
40,000 : 1
ANS: 4
10. The leakage current in a crystal diode is due to ....
minority carriers
majority carriers
junction capacitance
none of the above
ANS: 1
11. If the temperature of a crystal diode increases, then leakage
current ....
remains the same
decreases
increases
becomes zero
ANS: 3
12. The PIV rating of a crystal diode is .... that of equivalent
vacuum diode
the same as
lower than
more than
none of the above
ANS: 2
13. If the doping level of a crystal diode is increased, the breakdown

voltage.............
remains the same
is increased
is decreased
none of the above
ANS: 3

14. The knee voltage of a crystal diode is approximately equal to ....
applied voltage
breakdown voltage
forward voltage
barrier potential
ANS: 4

15. When the graph between current through and voltage across a device is a straight line, the device is referred to as ....
linear
active
nonlinear
passive
ANS: 1

16. When the crystal current diode current is large, the bias is ....
forward
inverse
poor
reverse
ANS: 1

17. A crystal diode is a .... device
non-linear
bilateral
linear
none of the above
ANS: 1

18. A crystal diode utilises .... characteristic for rectification
reverse
forward
forward or reverse
none of the above
ANS: 2

19. When a crystal diode is used as a rectifier, the most important consideration is ....
forward characteristic
doping level
reverse characteristic
PIC rating
ANS: 4
20. If the doping level in a crystal diode is increased, the width of depletion layer...........
remains the same
is decreased
in increased
none of the above
ANS: 3
21. A zener diode has ....
one pn junction
two pn junctions
three pn junctions
none of the above
ANS: 1
22. A zener diode is used as ....
an amplifier
a voltage regulator
a rectifier
a multivibrator
ANS: 2
23. The doping level in a zener diode is .... that of a crystal diode
the same as
less than
more than
none of the above
ANS: 3
24. A zener diode is always .... connected.
reverse
forward
either reverse or forward
none of the above
ANS: 1

25. A zener diode utilizes .... characteristics for its operation.
forward
reverse
both forward and reverse
none of the above
ANS: 2
26. In the breakdown region, a zener didoe behaves like a .... source.
constant voltage
constant current
constant resistance
none of the above
ANS: 1
27. A zener diode is destroyed if it..............
is forward biased
is reverse biased
carrier more than rated current
none of the above
ANS: 3
28. A series resistance is connected in the zener circuit to...........
properly reverse bias the zener
protect the zener
properly forward bias the zener
none of the above
ANS: 2
29. A zener diode is .... device
a non-linear
a linear
an amplifying
none of the above
ANS: 1
30. A zener diode has .... breakdown voltage
undefined
sharp
zero
none of the above
ANS: 2
31. .... rectifier has the lowest forward resistance

solid state
vacuum tube
gas tube
none of the above
ANS: 1

32. Mains a.c. power is converrted into d.c. power for ....
lighting purposes
heaters
using in electronic equipment
none of the above
ANS: 3

33. The disadvantage of a half-wave rectifier is that the..................
components are expensive
diodes must have a higher power rating
output is difficult to filter
none of the above
ANS: 3

34. If the a.c. input to a half-wave rectifier is an r.m.s value of $400/\sqrt{2}$ volts, then diode PIV rating is ....
$400/\sqrt{2}$ V
400 V
$400 \times \sqrt{2}$ V
none of the above
ANS: 2

35. The ripple factor of a half-wave rectifier is ....
21
.21
2.5
0.48
ANS: 4

36. There is a need of transformer for ....
half-wave rectifier
centre-tap full-wave rectifier
bridge full-wave rectifier
none of the above
ANS: 2

37. The PIV rating of each diode in a bridge rectifier is .... that of the equivalent centre-tap rectifier

one-half
the same as
twice
four times
ANS: 1

38. For the same secondary voltage, the output voltage from a centretap rectifier is .... than that of bridge rectifier
twice
thrice
four time
one-half
ANS: 4

39. If the PIV rating of a diode is exceeded, ...
the diode conducts poorly
the diode is destroyed
the diode behaves like a zener diode
none of the above
ANS: 2

40. A 10 V power supply would use .... as filter capacitor.
paper capacitor
mica capacitor
electrolytic capacitor
air capacitor
ANS: 3

41. A 1,000 V power supply would use .... as a filter capacitor
paper capacitor
air capacitor
mica capacitor
electrolytic capacitor
ANS: 1

42. The .... filter circuit results in the best voltage regulation
choke input
capacitor input
resistance input
none of the above
ANS: 1

43. A half-wave rectifier has an input voltage of 240 V r.m.s. If the step-down transformer has a turns ratio of 8:1, what is the peak load

voltage? Ignore diode drop.

27.5 V

86.5 V

30 V

42.5 V

ANS: 4

44. The maximum efficiency of a half-wave rectifier is ....

40.6 %

81.2 %

50 %

25 %

ANS: 1

45. The most widely used rectifier is ....

half-wave rectifier

centre-tap full-wave rectifier

bridge full-wave rectifier

none of the above

ANS:3

1. A transistor has ....

A] one pn junction

B] two pn junctions

C] three pn junctions

D] four pn junctions

2. The number of depletion layers in a transistor is ....

A] four

B] three

C] one

D] two

3. The base of a transistor is .... doped

A] heavily

B] moderately

C] lightly

D] none of the above

4. The element that has the biggest size in a transistor is ....

A] collector

B] base

C] emitter

D] collector-base-junction

5. In a pnp transistor, the current carriers are ....
A] acceptor ions
B] donor ions
C] free electrons
D] holes
6. The collector of a transistor is .... doped
A] heavily
B] moderately
C] lightly
D] none of the above
7. A transistor is a .... operated device
A] current
B] voltage
C] both voltage and current
D] none of the above
8. In a npn transistor, ... are the minority carriers
A] free electrons
B] holes
C] donor ions
D] acceptor ions
9. The emitter of a transistor is .... doped
A] lightly
B] heavily
C] moderately
D] none of the above
10. In a transistor, the base current is about .... of emitter current
A] 25%
B] 20%
C] 35 %
D] 5%
11. At the base-emitter junctions of a transistor, one finds ....
A] a reverse bias
B] a wide depletion layer
C] low resistance
D] none of the above
12. The input impedance of a transistor is ....
A] high
B] low

C] very high
D] almost zero
13. Most of the majority carriers from the emitter ....
A] recombine in the base
B] recombine in the emitter
C] pass through the base region to the collector
D] none of the above
14. The current IB is ....
A] electron current
B] hole current
C] donor ion current
D] acceptor ion current
15. In a transistor ....
A] IC = IE + IB
B] IB = IC + IE
C] IE = IC – IB
D] IE = IC + IB
16. The value of a of a transistor is ....
A] more than 1
B] less than 1
C] 1
D] none of the above
17. IC = aIE + ...
A] IB
B] ICEO
C] ICBO
D] ßIB
18. The output impedance of a transistor is ....
A] high
B] zero
C] low
D] very low
19. In a tansistor, IC = 100 mA and IE = 100.2 mA. The value of ß is ....
A] 100
B] 50
C] about 1
D] 200

20. In a transistor if ß = 100 and collector current is 10 mA, then IE is ....

A] 100 mA

B] 100.1 mA

C] 110 mA

D] none of the above

21. The relation between ß and a is ....

A] ß = 1 / (1 – a)

B] ß = (1 – a) / a

C] ß = a / (1 – a)

D] ß = a / (1 + a)

22. The value of ß for a transistor is generally ....

A] 1less than 1

B] between 20 and 500

C] above 500

23. The most commonly used transistor arrangement is .... arrangement

A] common emitter

B] common base

C] common collector

D] none of the above

24. The input impedance of a transistor connected in ....arrangement is the highest

A] common emitter

B] common collector

C] common base

D] none of the above

25. The output impedance of a transistor connected in ....

A] arrangement is the highest

B] common emitter

C] common collector

D] common base

none of the above

26. The phase difference between the input and output voltages in a common base arrangement is ....

A] 180o

B] 90o

C] 270o

D] <u>0o</u>

27. The power gain in a transistor connected in .... arrangement is the highest

A] <u>common emitter</u>

B] common base

C] common collector

D] none of the above

28. The phase difference between the input and output voltages of a transistor connected in common emitter arrangement is ....

A] 0o

B] <u>180o</u>

C] 90o

D] 270o

29. The voltage gain in a transistor connected in .... arrangement is the highest

A] common base

B] common collector

C] <u>common emitter</u>

D] none of the above

30. As the temperature of a transistor goes up, the base-emitter resistance ....

A] <u>decreases</u>

B] increases

C] remains the same

D] none of the above

31. The voltage gain of a transistor connected in common collector

A] arrangement is ....

B] equal to 1

C] more than 10

D] <u>more than 100 less than 1</u>

32. The phase difference between the input and output voltages of a transistor connected in common collector arrangement is ....

A] 180o

B] <u>0o</u>

C] 90o

D] 270o

33. IC = ß IB + ...

A] ICBO

B] IC
C] ICEO
D] aIE
34. IC = [a / (1 – a)] IB + ...
A] ICEO
B] ICBO
C] IC
D] (1 – a) IB
35. IC = [a / (1 – a)] IB + [........ / (1 – a)]
A] ICBO
B] ICEO
C] IC
D] IE
36. BC 147 transistor indicates that it is made of ....
A] germanium
B] silicon
C] carbon
D] none of the above
37. ICEO = (.........) ICBO
A] ß1
B] + a
C] 1 + ß
D] none of the above
38. A transistor is connected in CB mode. If it is not connected in CE mode with same bias voltages, the values of IE, IB and IC will ....
A] remain the same
B] increase
C] decrease
D] none of the above
39. If the value of a is 0.9, then value of ß is ....
A] 9
B] 0.9
C] 900
D] 90
40. In a transistor, signal is transferred from a .... circuit
A] high resistance to low resistance
B] low resistance to high resistance
C] high resistance to high resistance

D] low resistance to low resistance

41. The arrow in the symbol of a transistor indicates the direction of ....

A] electron current in the emitter

B] electron current in the collector

C] hole current in the emitter

D] donor ion current

42. The leakage current in CE arrangement is .... that in CB arrangement

A] more than

B] less than

C] the same as

D] none of the above

43. A heat sink is generally used with a transistor to ....

A] increase the forward current

B] decrease the forward current

C] compensate for excessive doping

D] prevent excessive temperature rise

44. The most commonly used semiconductor in the manufacture of a transistor is ....

A] germanium

B] silicon

C] carbon

D] none of the above

45. The collector-base junction in a transistor has ....

A] forward bias at all times

B] reverse bias at all times

C] low resistance

D] none of the above

1 : What is pickling process?

A : Buffing

B : Cleaning

C : Polishing

D : Roughening

2 : Which acid is used for pickling of mild steel?

A : Hydrochloric acid

B : Nitric acid

C : Sulphonic acid

D : Hydrofluoric acid

3 : Which power source is used in electroplating?

A : AC

B : Low DC

C : High AC

D : High DC

4 : Which is removed on metals by using acid pickling?

A : Oxide

B : Paints

C : Oil

D : Grease

5 : What is the unit of current density in electroplating?

A : Amp/ m2

B : Amp/Second

C : Amp/m

D : Amp/ Voltage

6 : Which depends on mass deposited as per Faraday's laws of electrolysis?

A : Current

B : Time

C : Current and Time

D : Voltage

7 : Which law is applied for electroplating?

A : Faraday's law of electrolysis

B : Ohm's law

C : Lenz's law

D : Kirchoff's law

8 : What is the molecular weight of water?

A : 18g/mol

B : 20g/mol

C : 17g/mol

D : 16g/mol

9 : What is the unit of molecular weight?

A : g/mol

B : gm/l

C : gram

D : kilogram

10 : Which solution the solute concentration is lower?

A : Saturated solution

B : Unsaturated solution

C : Super saturated solution

D : Normal solution

11 : Which is the example of soft water?

A : Drinking water

B : Rain

C : Soap water

D : Salt water

12 : Which is the name of material used for tank lining in electroplating?

A : Rubber

B : Wood

C : PVC

D : Plastic

13 : Which type of cleaning, spray cleaning comes under?

A : Preliminary cleaning

B : Final cleaning

C : Chemical cleaning

D : Bright dipping

14 : Which process follows polishing in electroplating?

A : Drying

B : Buffing

C : Deburring

D : De-Scaling

15 : Which is the other name of abrasive finishing in electroplating?

A : Crossing

B : Polishing

C : Buffing

D : Drying

16 : Which is the name of process that cleaning the metal in acid to remove corrosion

products from the surface?

A : Pickling

B : De-scaling

C : Drying

D : Deburring

17 : Which is the equivalent weight of oxalic acid crystals?

A : 53

B : 58
C : 61
D : 63
18 : Which acid is used for pickling and etching of metal?
A : Sulphuric acid
B : Boric acid
C : Phosphoric acid
D : Phosphorus acid
19 : Which chemical is used for vapour degreasing?
A : Trichloroethylene
B : Sodium carbonate
C : Trisodium phosphate
D : Sodium hydroxide
20 : Which solution is used for alkaline cleaning?
A : Sodium carbonate
B : Trichloroethylene
C : Ammonium citrate
D : Sodium chloride
21 : Which solution is used for pickling of ferrous metal?
A : Hcl acid solution
B : HF acid solution
C : HNO3 acid solution
D : H2 SO4 acid solution
22 : Which solution is used for pickling of non-ferrous metals?
A : H2SO4 acid solution
B : HF acid solution
C : Nitric acid solution
D : Hcl acid solution
23 : Which solution is used for pickling of magnesium alloys?
A : Hydrochloric acid solution
B : Hydrofluoric acid solution
C : Nitric acid solution
D : Dilute sulphuric acid
24 : Which method is used to maintain nickel bath?
A : LOD metric method
B : Titrations
C : EDTA Method
D : Gravity method

25 : Which material is used for masking of hard plating?
A : Stopping off lacquer
B : PVC tapes
C : Araldite
D : Glue
26 : Which tank is used for copper plating?
A : Plain welded steel
B : Lead line tank
C : Glass line tank
D : Antimonial lead line tank
27 : What is the atomic number of copper?
A : 30
B : 29
C : 28
D : 31
28 : What is the temperature of acid copper solution?
A : 60 to 71°C
B : 40 to 45°C
C : 45 to 55°C
D : 25 to 30°C
29 : Which type heater is suitable for acid copper solution?
A : Steel case electric immersion heater
B : Silica case heater
C : Lead line heater
D : Glass line immersion heater
30 : What is rochelle copper salt?
A : Cyanide copper salt
B : Acid copper salt
C : Usex copper salt
D : Copper fluaborak salt
31 : Which cyanide salt is used for copper plating?
A : Acid copper salt
B : Rochelle copper salt
C : Usex copper salt
D : Copper fluo salt
32 : Which type solution is used for copper plating removal by immersion method?
A : Chromic acid and Sulphuric acid

B : Nitric acid and Hydrochloric acid

C : Fier salt and Hydrochronic acid

D : Hydro fluoric acid and Cyanide solution

33 : Which is the property of nickel?

A : Rapid soluble in hydrochloride

B : High mechanical strength

C : Dilute sulphuric acid attacks nickel

D : Low mechanical strength

34 : Which type of electroplating is used for decorative finishing?

A : Gold plating

B : Silver plating

C : Nickel plating

D : Cadmium plating

35 : Which type of plating tank is used for swilling, drag in and drag out operation for nickel

plating?

A : Glass fibre tank

B : Enamelled tank

C : Stoneware tank

D : Stainless steel tank

36 : What are the chemical contains in electrolyte used for dull nickel plating?

A : Nickel chloride, Boric acid and Ammonium sulphate

B : Boric acid, Nickel sulphate and Ammonium chloride

C : Dilute sulphuric acid, Hydro chloric acid and Boric acid

D : Nickel sulphate, Sulphuric acid and Hydrochloride

37 : What is the range of pH value is to be maintained for nickel plating solution?

A : 2.5 to 3.0

B : 3.2 to 4.2

C : 3.6 to 4.2

D : 4.5 to 5.0

38 : Which metal is used to remove the organic impurities from nickel plating solution?

A : Silver

B : Carbon

C : Nichrome

D : Chromium

39 : What is the name of the defect occurs due to excessive current density?

A : Imperfect adhesion

B : Rough and dark deposit

C : Black (or) dark plating

D : Pitting of deposit

40 : What is the name of the defect of nickel plating?

A : Blistered

B : Uncoated

C : Pitted

D : Semi bright

41 : Which metal, the nickel deposit can be removed by electrolytic process?

A : Zinc base alloys

B : Copper base alloys

C : Chromium base alloys

D : Silver base alloys

42 : Which precaution is essential for effective adherence of chromium deposit on the

surface to be electroplated?

A : Should be in rectangular shape

B : Should be in clean condition

C : Should be flat

D : Should have more thickness

43 : What is the use of bright chromium plating?

A : For articles with brilliant bluish white appearance

B : In electronics and semi conductor device

C : For decorative coating iron and steel

D : For electric utility to artistic sculptures

44 : What is the purpose of polypropylene tank used for bright chromium plating?

A : To reduce spray and the loss of solution

B : For swilling drag in and drag out

C : To reduce the chromium solution filled in it

D : To reduce heat and evaporation losses

45 : How the chromium plating solution to extent it's grade to 100g/1000 AH?

A : By adding of high grade sulphuric acid

B : By adding of high grade chromic acid

C : By adding of chromium sulphate

D : By heating the solution upto 50°C temperature

46 : Which is the effect, due to the formation of trivalent chromium content with solution in

bright chromium plating?

A : Rise in temperature to high value

B : Fall in solution efficiency

C : Rise in concentration of chromic acid

D : Reduce the corrosion resistance

47 : Where the conventional bright chromium plating type is employed?

A : Electronic components

B : Automobile fitting

C : Electrical contacts

D : Flatware industries

48 : Which is used for the suspension of articles to be bright chromium plated?

A : Bus bars

B : Steel iron rods

C : Jigs (or) Racks

D : Iron angles

49 : Which defect occurs due to inefficient contacts of articles in bright chromium plating?

A : Brown stains on deposit

B : Dull, grey, rough deposit

C : Blistered deposits

D : Little chromium deposit on the article

50 : Which type of plating is applied for rotating mechanical parts?

A : Bright chromium plating

B : Hard chromium plating

C : Brass plating

D : Copper plating

51 : What is the range value of chromic acid used for high speed hard chromium plating

solution?

A : 100 g/l to 150 g/l

B : 200 g/l to 225 g/l

C : 250 g/l to 300 g/l

D : 300 g/l to 325 g/l

52 : Which process is used to reduce the chromium solution carried over on plated components?

A : Final rinsing

B : Post treatment

C : Neutralising dip

D : Heat treatment

53 : Which is the cause for soft deposit defect in hard chromium plating?

A : High current density

B : Too high temperature

C : Presence of grease

D : Too low current density

54 : Which acid is used to remove chromium from copper and its alloys?

A : Dilute sulphuric acid

B : Dilute hydrochloric acid

C : Cadmium cyanide

D : Sodium cyanide

ANSWERS :

1:B; 2:A; 3:B; 4:A; 5:A; 6:C; 7:A; 8:A; 9:A; 10:C; 11:B; 12:A; 13:C; 14:B; 15:A; 16:A; 17:D;

18:A; 19:A; 20:A; 21:A; 22:B; 23:D; 24:C; 25:A; 26:A; 27:B; 28:A; 29:A; 30:B; 31:C; 32:A; 33:B;

34:C; 35:D; 36:A; 37:C; 38:B; 39:B; 40:A; 41:B; 42:B; 43:A; 44:B; 45:B; 46:B; 47:B; 48:C; 49:A;

50:B; 51:C; 52:C; 53:D; 54:B;

www.ingramcontent.com/pod-product-compliance
Ingram Content Group UK Ltd.
Pitfield, Milton Keynes, MK11 3LW, UK
UKHW021917190726
13853UKWH00002B/710